Marlene Ellis
January 1974.

AFRICAN HARVEST

HILARY RUBEN

AFRICAN HARVEST

HARVILL PRESS, LONDON

The author wishes to thank Routledge & Kegan Paul Ltd for permission to quote from *The Samburu* by Paul Spencer, and Putnam & Company Ltd for permission to quote from *Out of Africa* by Karen Blixen (Isak Dinesen).

ISBN 0 00 272003 5
© Hilary Ruben 1972
Made and Printed in Great Britain by
William Collins Sons & Co Ltd, Glasgow,
for the publishers Harvill Press Limited,
30A Pavilion Road, London SW1

*For Monty, and for Lissa and Mandy,
all of whom were born in this country*

Contents

Introduction ... 11

CIRCLE I
Home and Just Beyond ... 13

CIRCLE II
Peter's Camp, the Ngong Hills and the Masai Wells ... 45

CIRCLE III
Into the Bush ... 67

CIRCLE IV
The Diminishing Band ... 82

CIRCLE V
The Elephant and Us ... 102

CIRCLE VI
Baharini ... 131

CIRCLE VII
The Nomads and the Stone Deserts of the North ... 148

Return to Marsabit ... 176

Glossary of Swahili Words ... 191

Illustrations

between pages 48 and 49

An early morning stroll in the garden
Hilary Ruben

Mandy and Northey Chongo, the vervet monkey
Peter Beard

Lissa and Mitzi, the bush baby
Hilary Ruben

A Masai boy on the slopes between the Ngong Hills and the Masai Wells
Monty Ruben

Dusk at Naivasha
Hilary Ruben

Masai women intrigued by Lissa's and Mandy's hair
Monty Ruben

between pages 160 and 161

The author at Lake Nakuru
Lissa Ruben

Monty and Mandy on safari
Hilary Ruben

Mandy's first meeting with the Samburu girls
Jean-Jacques Manigot

Smiles and laughter made their own language
Hilary Ruben

ILLUSTRATIONS

Elephants on the march
Monty Ruben

Leopard at Serengeti
Mandy Ruben

The trailer carrying the boat across the stone deserts of the north
Monty Ruben

Endpaper: 'Dawn in the bush'
Mandy Ruben

Introduction

OFTEN since I arrived in this country I have found myself wishing that I were an artist instead of a writer, for the beauty of colour and light and form vary from the red earth of the Kikuyu soil to the indigo sea of the Bajun fishermen; from the fragile grace of a thorn tree to the craggy hulk of an elephant; from sun-steeped plains and honey-brown grass to the scarlet petal of a cactus flower and the snowy peaks of Kerinyaga.

Perhaps it was in a moment of rebellion against words, or in a mood of dissatisfaction with them, that this book occurred to me in the form of a symbol. It was very simple: a series of circles one within the other in which the outermost circumference passed through the desert and the sea and the innermost encompassed the miniature world of the garden. Lines radiating from the centre represented the threads of a family woven through the rich tapestry of their environment, and the central point itself symbolized our home.

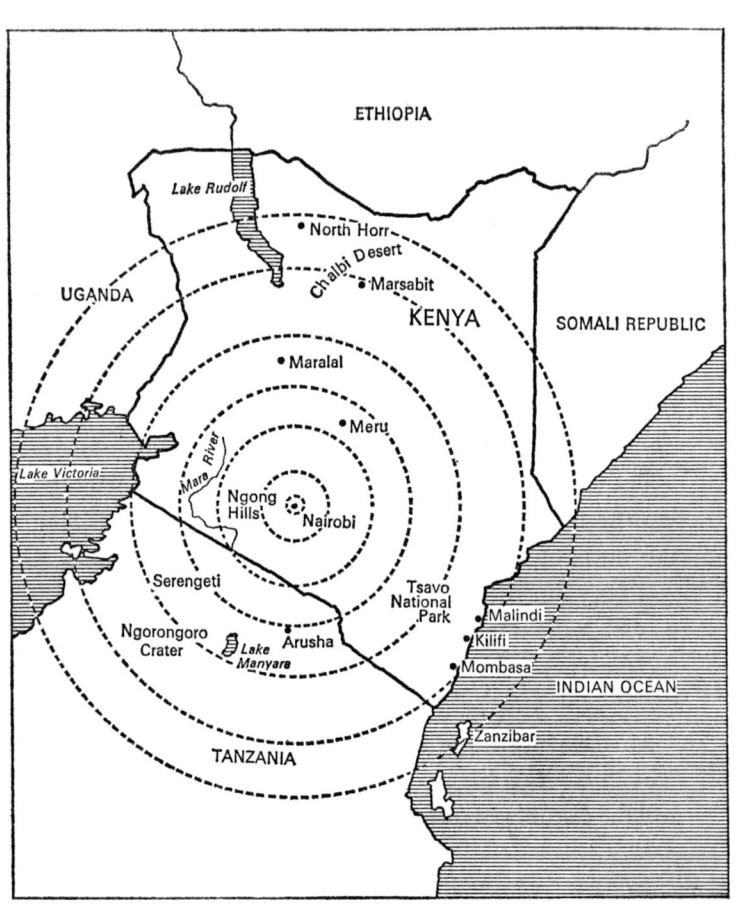

CIRCLE I

Home and Just Beyond

THE old world of the tribalist beat with its slow, steady rhythm on one side of my new home, while the new, hectic world of the twentieth century rushed forward to meet it on the other. The Kikuyu village half a mile up the road still lay steeped in traditions practised hundreds of years ago, but the town six miles away in the other direction had leapt up in half a century.

Time in Africa is not the same as in the West: either it moves like a wide, slow river – like the Galana, like the Ouasa Nyiro – or it rushes with the uncontrolled turbulence of a mighty waterfall. Ten years may be the equivalent of a century elsewhere, or a thousand years may pass unmarked by any of the changes in the outside world. Democracy has followed on the heels of tribalism in fifty years, yet there are many places within its demesne where only the cycle of hot, dry months followed by weeks of heavy rain indicates the passage of time, and an hour or a day, or even a year, is of little consequence.

Changes and developments in our own lives have taken place in synchronization with the changes in the country around us: my husband Monty was born here, in the colonial era; I arrived at a time of violence, just as it was ending.

Outwardly, all seemed calm and beautiful enough. The four great jacaranda trees that surround the house were in full bloom and blossoms hung low over the roof like a lilac cloud. Lines of coffee closed in on my new home like a dark green ruff, a clump of banana trees amongst them and a few mimosa saplings. From the bedroom veranda I could see the four humps of the Ngong Hills and further away, much further away, the snowy peaks of Kerinyaga. But the peaceful beauty was deceptive, for it was October 1952, and the beginning of Mau Mau.

The State of Emergency was declared the same week that we came to this house. I cannot say that I was often afraid or even that it was Mau Mau itself that made those early days so difficult; it was simply the barrier that it formed between me and my new environment. In the evenings, Monty placed his gun beside his plate in case one of the two servants opened the door to a gang of terrorists. I neither liked nor trusted these two men. Their faces seemed to me like two black masks which concealed their every thought and feeling, and as I could not yet speak Swahili, there was no means of changing this impression. The massacre of an entire village twenty miles away and the mutilated bodies of four Africans half a mile up the road didn't help matters, any more than the gun Monty insisted I carry with me in a holster. On alternate nights, Monty was out with the police helping patrol the area and often he would not return until the early hours of the morning. We had no telephone in those days and we could not yet afford a second car so that I felt cut off from any means of help should I require it. I am an optimist by nature and did not expect to require it – even so, there were nights when some unidentified sound caused me to start listening and, once I began, it was impossible to stop; the hours till Monty's return seemed to pass then in a series of rigid, staccato seconds. I felt much further away than I would normally have done from the Buckinghamshire countryside where I spent my childhood, from shopping in

CIRCLE I

Knightsbridge, or from the American university where I was studying at the time I met Monty.

I didn't have to stay in the house alone. I could, had I chosen, have banded together with other women who collected in one or other of their homes while their husbands were out on patrol. But the idea held no appeal for me and I made up my mind that if I were going to live in this country I would live as normal a life as possible – or go back to England.

It was green, this place he brought me to, and beyond the coffee clad slopes surrounding us were forests and pine trees and hills that reminded me of Scotland. But once we hit the great spaces and warm, tawny tones that I was later to love so much, I found myself longing for the familiar intimacy of hedged fields and thatched cottages. There were times when it all felt quite unreal, especially when the women came to pick our few acres of coffee and I found myself surrounded by a group of dusky women in cotton sarongs, their heads shaved, their ear lobes stretched and knotted. It was my duty to pay them according to their pickings when they finished work, usually around three in the afternoon. The sun beat down on the hot earth and the mounds of berries with their pungent, slightly acrid smell; the women laughed and chatted in unfamiliar Kikuyu accents. Against my side, its weight a constant reminder of hostility, was that gun. As long as I carried it, it was impossible for me to begin any satisfactory relationship with this new country and the people who inhabited it.

In another way, this was not an easy time for Monty either. It was not a matter of adjustment as he had been born in this country and his father and mother had come here as children. They, and his grandparents too, belonged to that little band of pioneers who struggled to create a better life for themselves, to develop farms from unbroken soil and to build a city from a couple of *dukas* and a muddy street. Monty spoke Swahili before he spoke English, he went to school here, he worked for six months on the farm his father once owned high in the hills, and he served in the war with African troops. No, it was not a matter of adjustment; it was, basically, a matter of colonial policy. After the war, he had gone to London University and graduated in Zoology. When we returned here soon after we were married, he found that for some strange bureaucratic reason the Government preferred recruiting personnel through the Colonial Office in London to employing suitably qualified locals. There were a couple of jobs available, but these were deep in the heart of the bush and our first child was about to be born. He refused the offers and went into commerce instead.

I am firmly convinced it makes little difference whether we turn left or right in life, the same number of positive results will accrue, the same number of negative, for the special characteristics inherent in us will in any case attract or repel certain types of events. And so although Monty is not primarily a businessman at heart, nor money nor material possessions his prime motivation, and if a certain perceptiveness and understanding and clarity of thought might have been put to better use, there have been other opportunities and advantages of which a few are only making themselves apparent now. They developed slowly, like the family, like the garden, like the house. And like my own groping adjustments to the environment in which I found myself.

Perhaps the first step forward was when I discarded the gun. It was still the early days of the Emergency, but if I objected to it as a symbol of hatred, it also happened to be more of a danger than a protection to me. Not because I couldn't shoot – I

CIRCLE I

enjoyed target practice and was becoming quite proficient at it – but because I am very forgetful and the penalty for losing a gun was a fine of up to two hundred and fifty pounds, and an uneasy conscience: the weapon would certainly make its way into the hands of the Mau Mau. The excuse was valid, I discarded my holster and a bull terrier pup destined to a short but vigorous life gambolled at my heels instead. Perhaps it would have been difficult for me to be really happy wherever I was living at that time; perhaps Mau Mau and growing pains had become a little confused in my mind so that I could not tell where one ended and the other began. Some people start growing up very quickly, some never start at all and some begin very late. I began very late. And I am not at all sure that the uncertainty and the chaos of the country, which like a Greek creation myth was waiting to be arranged and formed, was not a reflection of what I vaguely felt myself.

One of the happiest occasions was when Monty took me to the coast for the first time: the fresh, sweet taste of mangoes in the sun, the hot sand beneath my feet, the coconut palms and the dhows. We surfed and we swam and we lazed in the sun; we wandered along the sleepy, dilapidated streets of Malindi where Vasco da Gama once trod. An itinerant camel, I remember, wandered with us, and on a post behind the colourful mounds of fruits a monkey chattered incessantly.

We went home, back to everyday life and the State of Emergency. It would continue for some years to come and several years would pass before I made my first African friends and began to understand Mau Mau – amongst other things – from another point of view. It would be some time too before the first Kikuyu* authors appeared to emphasize the fact that if

* Correctly 'Gikuyu' but usually spelt 'Kikuyu' by Europeans.

politics had been one of the causes, the central and explosive issue was land; the good earth so dear to the heart of a Kikuyu and his passionate desire to wrest it back from what he believed to be the European's unfair possession of it.

Meantime there were other changes. Monty and Kamau the gardener pulled out the first few coffee trees and planted in their place the first few feet of lawn. They began too their long struggle with the couch grass and the bush, and as it slowly disappeared, hibiscus and frangipani and oleander began to bloom. Scarlet bells cascaded from the branches of the two Australian flames and a family of woodpeckers made their home in the makuruwe tree. Eucalyptus seedlings thrust their heads towards the clouds and bamboo shoots were erupting into thickets; soon Kerinyaga and the Ngong Hills would be lost to view. Perhaps in life the key word is growth. Be it a garden or a child or a work of art, there is in this development a deep satisfaction and a *raison d'être*. It was good to watch the creepers pushing across the bare walls, to pick the first fruits of the avocado tree, to watch the first mangoes appear and the first guavas. But the garden was Monty's forte, and beside the couch grass and the bush, he had to struggle with Kamau's stubbornness and my own horticultural inadequacy. I have not the patience for it.

Now too I could speak Swahili, Kenya's lingua franca. Almost as important, my two original servants had been dismissed and I had working for me an old man and a young boy. The old man was a Jaluo from the shores of Lake Victoria. He moved slowly and his face was kindly; he was simple and dignified, slow-witted yet wise with a wisdom that was basic and earthy. He put up with my impatience, I with his slowness in work and comprehension of a world not his own. I began to read a little about the tribes. When first I made reference to tribal customs or beliefs of which the Wazungu (Europeans) were deemed to be totally ignorant, both Mika and Kamau smiled incredulously. They began to talk to me then. Mika told me that formerly all the African people believed the sun was God; then the Luo discovered there was only one God and that he was formless and invisible (the Shilluk of the Sudan, ancestors of the Luo, call this invisible form Juok). He was convinced of the truth and superiority of Christianity because it was '*written in a book*'; but he disapproved of Catholic missionaries in particular 'because they prayed to statues' and missionaries in general because when he was a boy they only taught religious knowledge. He was not totally naïve.

Paulo, the young boy, was a Mkamaba. Part of the time he helped me in the kitchen, and the rest of the time he sat in the sun strumming his guitar. It should have been a flute for he had a heart-shaped face and slanting eyes and a grin like Pan's. He was dreamy and forgetful, lazy and imaginative; when for the first time we took him to the coast, he was so affected by the beauty of the sea, so filled with wonder at its vastness, he neither heard us when we spoke to him nor was capable of any work. He would stand leaning on his broom, staring out at the horizon, in a sort of trance. Probably a little 'pot' (which grows in this country almost as easily as couch grass) sent the bubbles of his dreams floating even higher. Infected by the restlessness of the sea and inflamed by it with a desire to see the world, he disappeared with his guitar into the heart of the Congo. Whether fate threw him into the hands of mercenaries or cannibals, or whether he married a Congo maid, or whether perhaps he pushed southwards to the diamond mines and the gold, we have never heard.

As for Mika, he is living in retirement at his home on the shores of Lake Victoria. Kamau the gardener of course is with us still; it is impossible to imagine the garden without him.

*

Kamau ambled into our lives with his flat-footed, bandy-legged gait almost sixteen years ago, when first we came to this house. He is as much a part of the garden as the bamboo thickets and the banana trees; when he works in the sunshine and the stillness of the afternoon his rhythm is as attuned to the elements as the regular click of his shears or the tapping of his *panga* on the earth. Honest and good-natured, his long, ugly face is frequently split by a smile that spills into every crease and brims over into the small, kind eyes. His ear lobes have been stretched to form two loops, one of which he neatly knots while the other he leaves loose.

He is a little deaf and if you call out 'Jambo!' he might answer: 'Yes I will close the gate' or 'this morning I will weed the lawn.' But if you tell him to weed the lawn, he closes the gate, and this is not on account of his deafness at all. He has heard you perfectly well, but he is adamantly and perfectly contrary. He is also possessed of a great and clumsy strength; I could not break with a hammer things that Kamau has managed to break with his hands and this, combined with his contrariness and his deafness, can sometimes be highly infuriating. But it is useless upbraiding him. He will simply listen with infinite and sorrowful patience and then produce some irrefutable reason propounded from his own unique logic why he could not conceivably have acted in any other fashion.

CIRCLE I

But there is much about Kamau that is unique beside his logic – the way he weeds the lawn for example, sitting on the grass, plucking a blade here and a blade there like a woman tidying her eyebrows or cleaning a chicken, and when he wants to move, inching along on his bottom. He works barefoot and dressed in tatters: a pair of trousers overgrown with patches, a sweater that has shrunk to his chest and a dirty old piece of cloth wrapped round his head like a veritable pirate. The clothes that Monty has given him lie stored away in a box beneath his bed. I once asked him why. 'Memsabu,' he said with his slight stutter, 'if I wore them they would only get spoiled.'

Yet even Kamau cannot completely resist the influence of the new world that is springing up around him. Today he arrives and leaves in a tweed jacket and an unpatched pair of khaki pants. His huge feet though are encompassed in some form of rubber footwear he has made himself from an old tyre – sandals in the dry season and something resembling flippers in the wet. On his head he wears an ancient trilby hat and in his hand he carries a staff, like some mediaeval shepherd.

There is no autumn and there is no spring, but there is jacaranda time and mimosa, and the smell of the earth after the rain. There is also the time of the coffee. Twice a year it comes into bloom. It looks as though snow has fallen during the night and the air is filled with a pungent perfume, half bitter, half sweet. In the days when we struggled to cultivate our small holding of coffee, as soon as the sap inside the berries tasted honey-sweet, Kamau would call his female relatives from the village up the road, and the picking would begin. Singing and chattering, they would strip the berries from the branches and fill the plaited baskets hanging at their sides. Children helped too, and at the end of the day we would give them milk to drink and something to eat.

Twice during this time there was famine, yet never once did a child more than raise a thin arm towards the food, never once clamour nor grab – and one might have expected it in the circumstances, for they were hungry. Yet one Christmas when I appeared with my two daughters, Lissa and Mandy, with armfuls of toys, we were mobbed by an excited, screaming crowd of grown boys and women. Seizing the dolls from us, the women rocked them against their breasts and with great merriment pretended to suckle them; the boys held them aloft, delighted with eyes that opened and closed and strange little voices that cried out 'Mamma, Mamma . . .' The small ones for whom the toys had been intended stood bewildered and empty-handed. Nor did their expressions change when Lissa and Mandy found spinning tops for them, building bricks and a musical box, for they had never seen such things and had to be taught how to use them.

Twice during the year Kamau's son has been sick. An evil eye had been cast upon him Kamau said, and adamantly rejecting European medicine, strode off in his home-made boots in search of the nearest witch-doctor. Kamau told me once that a man who coveted his land (land being the biggest bone of contention amongst the Kikuyu themselves as well as between the white man and the Kikuyu) offered him poisoned beer to drink. As a result of a spell cast upon him by a witch-doctor, Kamau was not affected by the deadly brew – but his evil host had met with sudden death instead. He added: 'Memsabu, if you wish, I can take you to see this *mganga* and he can cast a similar spell on you, so that you too will be safe from poisoned drinks.' I accepted this kind offer with alacrity. I had

CIRCLE I

long wanted to meet a witch-doctor (how enemies of Caligula or Tiberius would have appreciated such a man's services!) and I was disappointed when he moved on (he is an itinerant) before I had the chance to make his acquaintance. But he will return, Kamau assures me, and I will have the chance again. He had better come soon because the government doesn't approve of witch-doctors and they will soon be banished to the realms of European witches and sorcerers.

Kamau's son recovered, just as many men have recovered by their faith in God or a healer strong enough. But Kamau's remedies are not all a matter of faith: he can tell you which roots or leaves to brew in order to cure a cough or a fit of madness or a cold in the head.

When he was a small boy, he says, a *mganga* rubbed bee larvae pulp into his body because he was allergic to bee stings. (He wanted Mandy to undergo the same treatment for she is similarly sensitive.) A few years ago it so happened that a swarm of bees attacked Kamau while he was mowing the lawn. He received numerous stings and the rubber handles of the mower looked like pin cushions. African bees are known for their fierceness, yet Kamau was no more harmed by them than he had been by the poisoned beer.

A European friend of ours, to show his scorn of such powers, once jumped on an evil spell brewed by one of his farmhands. The old labourer cried out in horror, for the concoction had been intended to harm another of the farmhands and not his employer. But it was too late. The next day, stepping in exactly the same place where he had contemptuously trodden the spell underfoot, a sharp tool he was carrying in his basket gashed his leg. The wound required several stitches, it also turned septic and took six months to heal.

There are countless far stranger stories than these. Mostly they are dismissed with a shrug and banished to the realms of coincidence – where they are no bother to anyone. Usually, the greater the man's intellect the less easily can he countenance those phenomena which cannot be explained – partly because frequently the more the facts, the greater the blockage to some perception of any reality which may lie beyond that recognized by our everyday senses; partly because often such phenomena threaten the very structure of his thinking. The really rare mind combines both a large intellect and this type of perception as well. And so generally, with our Western scientific knowledge, we undermine African psychic knowledge and do not concede that if our own doctors know something the tribal doctors do not, the reverse applies also. In many cases, I think, a tribal doctor will use intuitive psychology – quite simply, understanding, which is the fundamental treatment of any patient and the reason why there are so few good GPs today (the old rural doctors were better) – and even fewer good psychiatrists.

There are good witch-doctors and bad, and a bad witch-doctor can ruin a man's life – or even end it if he wishes. Kamau told me that an old man, skeleton thin and rheumy eyed, who wanders along the road between here and the village, was bewitched into forgetting his home and his land. The *mganga* has commandeered the old man's land and the victim, I suppose, will wander till the day he dies. With a Frenchman it is an *affaire de cœur*, with a Kikuyu it is an *affaire de terre*. With Kamau it is both: he has three wives (which suggests his ragged appearance belies his wealth) and two plots of land. One plot of land is a hundred miles away, looked after by one of the wives, and the other is his family land inherited from his father; this lies half a mile up the road beyond the marsh.

The marsh is like a bird sanctuary, kavirondo crested cranes and hammer-headed storks frequent the swampy grass, wild geese and glossy ibis. The girls like to walk there, and in the rainy season we go each day to see if the level of the water has risen yet to the level of the road; during the long rains in April and May, and the short ones in October, water runs down the surrounding hillsides and the marsh fills like a bowl. Ducks float across the surface and at night there is the thunderous croaking of a thousand frogs. Twice the marsh has brimmed over the road and turned our garden into a lake, killing pawpaw and mango trees and leaving acacia seedlings and tobacco plants in its wake. Every rainy season the road leading to the house used to turn into a quagmire and there were days – to their delight – when the girls couldn't go to school. Now the road has been macadamized, although it's just as narrow, and we have dug a miniature canal to divert the waters of the flooding marsh.

Winding slightly uphill between the coffee trees, the road leads to a village. There are round huts of mud and thatch, the hillsides are patched with clumps of banana trees and ragged squares of maize; the earth is red, the hills are green, and a stream winds through every valley. Kamau's other two wives weed and plant the soil, chop wood and fetch water. We often see them with other women from the village, trotting along the road between the house and the marsh carrying heavy loads of wood hanging from a headstrap. Their backs are bent and their eyes cast down, but if you call a greeting even the oldest of them, old long before her time, will glance up from under her eyebrows with a warm response and a wide smile.

Each wife, in accordance with Kikuyu custom, has a hut of her own, for there are men's affairs and there are women's affairs and each needs a place of their own to conduct them accordingly; each too has need of a little privacy. They work hard, these women, for diligence is the key word of the Kikuyu tribe. And if they take second place when they are young, old age will bring them honour and respect – of which they will take full advantage for Kikuyu women can be dominating and strong! Perhaps they cannot forget that their tribe, so the legend goes, originated in a matriarchy led by nine women. But one day the nine husbands of the nine wives conspired and made all the women fall pregnant at the same time. Then, when the women were at their weakest and all were heavy with child, the men took advantage of their condition and wrenched their power away from them. . . .

While the lives of the village women have changed little, their children and grandchildren have one foot in the new world, one in the old. Some have been in contact with missionaries, all go to missionary or government schools. Education is the most precious prize so that there was bitter feeling against the British not only because they did not provide a great deal more, but also because they closed down the schools started by the Kikuyu themselves at the outbreak of Mau Mau. Since Independence five years ago, the number of schools has been trebled. The children in the village up the road may only succeed in obtaining two or three years of education, but it is sufficient time for them to learn to write and read. Some have struggled right through primary into secondary, and it is a very hard struggle indeed. If they scrape enough money together to pay the fees (the country is still too young and too poor for free education) then perhaps they cannot afford a candle at night to work by; certainly most of them will have to walk several miles and back each day. Lucy is one such child.

The girls and I first met Lucy while walking past the marsh one day. A little girl in a bright cotton dress fell in step with us; she was slight and dainty with a heart-shaped face, a snub nose and a bright smile. She chattered away in staccato chirrups of English, like a bird. She knew our house well, she said, she had passed it often; wasn't it the one with the fierce dogs? She told us that she walked four miles to school each day and four miles back; that her father was dead and she had nine brothers and sisters.

'My mother,' she said, 'has so many children she is like a chicken with all its chicks. Yes, she is like a chicken with all its chicks!' Come and see us next time you pass the house, we said. Yes, she would like to come, but what about those dogs? Call Kamau, we said, he will come to the gate and let you in.

'I will come,' she promised, 'I know Kamau. I will come next Sunday and I will bring you some bananas and eggs.'

And she did. She has come often since, sometimes bearing a gift. It is touching, this African generosity; even the poorest like Lucy will find a few bananas on their small square of land, or an egg or two from the hen scratching the earth outside their hut to give you as a present. And when a Kikuyu receives a gift, the custom is to give a little sugar, or a little rice, in return.

Sometimes Kamau brings me a note from Lucy. I know then that something is wrong and she needs help, but is too shy to ask for it personally; she writes a letter instead. It always starts the same way and a little while ago I received one which ran like this:

Mguga Green Praimary School.
   Don't Don't forget me.
   Yours in maid,
Dear Mrs Ruben,
   Much greeting like stars in the sky. Much greeting from me and my mother and my sister. and How are you for many days my friend? after greeting I write to tell you that when I am going to school, the road which we are passing is closed and I must passes at Westlands and that is a very long way. Pleace may I be coming and be carrying by the woman who lives in your house? Please I asked you very kind. and much greeting from my mother and my sister theresa. ifen the baby has greeted you. greete Lissa's father, ifen yourself. Yours in maid, Lucy.

The track through the coffee farm had been closed by its owner and now she had to walk to school along the road; this added two miles to her journey. She knew – for Lucy from the beginning knew much more about us than we did about her – that Mandy was driven to school each morning at seven thirty by 'the woman who live in this house' (alias Nan) and she was, with her own sweet turn of phrase, begging the small favour of a lift.

Sometimes Lucy drops by with her eldest sister Theresa and a friend. Theresa is seventeen – or so she says; it is not the custom of unsophisticated Africans to count their birthdays and a tribalist knows only to which age group he belongs. She has a small baby but no husband; nor is she likely to find one, for now that she has the baby no man will marry her. She wants me to get her work – to get all her friends work – but she has no qualifications of any kind. She cannot even scrub a floor or make a bed (at this point Lucy assures me brightly that she is going to teach her to cook!). We sit on the lawn and drink tea, conversation dwindles. I have been learning a little Kikuyu; it is

CIRCLE I

difficult, ten classes of nouns, fifty-seven verb tenses. I utter a hesitant phrase or two: 'Please boil the potatoes. I am going to Nairobi. The children are in the garden.' (It reminds me of Spain, where all I could say was: no, no more flamencos, thank you, omelette and goodnight and *olé*.) The girls burst out laughing; it is incredible how you can change an atmosphere simply by saying a few words in somebody's native tongue.

They laugh easily these girls, but they have little to look forward to. They are the by-products of sudden change; they do not have a foot in two worlds, they have fallen into the no-man's land in between. They are outside the pale of tribalism and not yet within the pen of Protestantism; with the old rural ways disintegrating and the new urban ones still beyond their reach, they are the usual refugees left in the wake of rural defeat by a growing city. Social welfare, like free education, requires time and money. There are many such young people in the shanty town of Nairobi and for a couple of years I found myself in quite close contact with a few of them. To my intense surprise, I found myself teaching.

There were twenty girls in all, and the Salvation Army were providing them with a home and a minimum of education. An African friend told me they were desperate for an English teacher. Just an hour twice a week she said. But I became so involved the two hours stretched into four half-mornings. Their frame of reference was so cramped, their entire world so infinitely tiny! They did not even know that the world was round. Many of them had been no further than the mile that separated them from the shanty town in one direction and the city centre with its modern buildings in the other. It was difficult to make contact, impossible almost, but I enjoyed the challenge and I enjoyed too experimenting with different ways of holding their attention during class. They loved music and singing and so do I; with this at least in common we sometimes learned grammar by dance and syntax by song. One day I played Mozart for them to see their reaction. The music was totally foreign to them, a strange melody and an unknown beat. Yet after no more than twenty bars they were swaying in time to it and clapping their hands to the rhythm.

Sometimes I used to take them a step or two outside the tiny circle of their realm, show them wondrous things like machinery and lifts and the green hills beyond the city; or our own garden and the animals.

They were so silent when they came to spend the afternoon, and they talked in whispers when we went for a walk through the coffee. Did they enjoy themselves, Nan and I would ask one another afterwards? They were quiet as little brown mice, and they didn't eat either unless we disappeared from the room.

One day, one of the girls ran away from the Salvation Army Home. She was my best pupil, and the prettiest as well. I tracked her down to her 'home' in the shanty town: a tiny refuge large enough to hold a single bed, it was built of sacking and mud, cardboard and corrugated iron. Semi-naked children gathered round me on the dusty earth; the girl's older sister, just as pretty, but with an expression of lethargic acceptance in her eyes, leaned against a wall. Life has to have a direction, and in this shanty town there was none.

Before detribalization, these people had clearly defined codes by which they lived, and each of them belonged to an age group which would ostracize them if they transgressed the rules. Circumcision was one of the most important of all landmarks in their lives: it was a bridge from childhood to adulthood and both boys and girls looked forward to it with

CIRCLE I

joy and awe. Diligence, a key word amongst the Kikuyu, was impressed upon the initiate and he was made to understand the responsibilities that would soon be accorded him along with the privileges. At the ceremony, he would swear loyalty to other members of his age group, and to his clan. Laws against theft, murder and adultery were stringently defined as in the ten commandments, while honour of father and mother was emphasized by special forms of address expressing respect. It was also instilled in the candidate that he must bear himself with dignity and express his views modestly. It is a sad irony that the children governed by the very tribalism we have sought to wipe out in favour of our own way of life are amongst the best disciplined and well-mannered in the world, while some of the products of our own society are the very reverse.

The Kikuyu tribalist revered Ngai who dwelt upon Kerinyaga. He believed that the departed spirits of his ancestors dwelt not in heaven but in the earth beneath his family land and he behaved well in order to propitiate them. When a man left for the city he was no longer bound either by wrath or the pleasure of these spirits, or by censure from his age group. Nor could the lofty and frequently impractical teachings of Christianity – which he soon began to see few white men lived by – replace the way of life and the guide now lost to him.

The children in the shanty town have never known this way of life nor any of the traditions and customs which had splashed with colour the existence of their grandfathers. They are the forfeit paid for urbanity and sophistication.

My errant pupil appeared – I had half expected her to refuse to see me – eyes cast down and unkempt, she who had always been meticulously neat and clean. We went away from the children so that we could talk alone.

It doesn't help, when you are trying to reach a person, when you have to use a language that is neither yours nor theirs. (The girl was a Kikuyu and we spoke in Swahili.) I found myself confronted by a set expressionless face in which not even the quiver of a muscle betrayed I had touched a single feeling. As I talked, with no more than an occasional nod or shake of the head in response, I began to see that the Home was no more than a stopgap for these girls, it provided four years of security but no more hope for the future than when they left the shanty town.

Suddenly, a few tears rolled down the girl's cheek and at last she began to talk. She didn't want to go back to the Home, she wanted to stay in the shanty town. She didn't say so, but I knew that she was bored; the few weekly lessons, the bit of needlework were not sufficient to satisfy a mind that craved to learn. She cried too because she wanted desperately to go to school, but she had missed too many years and she would not be accepted. If she could not go to school, she preferred to share the one bed – or the floor – with her senile father and her five brothers and sisters. At least she would be sharing it with her own family. At least too there would be the daily happenings, the little joys, the eternal struggles, of the community. She would become a prostitute like her sister; what alternative was there? The Home would have found her work as a maid, but they could not find her companionship or friends.

It was depressing; she was an attractive girl with a bright mind, and had she been taken from her environment at six years old instead of twelve, she could have been an asset to the community instead of a parasite. But like most ghettos, there was no way out.

Before the girl and I both withdrew our presence from the

CIRCLE I

Home, I gave the class an essay to write in an attempt to find out the things I wanted to know which they would not tell. As usual, of all the essays, hers was easily the best, and I kept it. It runs as follows:

A STORY ABOUT SATURDAY

We live [leave] here on Saturday at four o clock. I was very happy to visit Mrs Ruben. We enjoy very much when we was there I was happy. because you take us for walk and I was happy to see that lovly house and those lovly flowers. and we enjoy very much. I was Happy for your tea. And the cakes. Everything that I saw it makes me very Happy. And also I was happy to rest in your lovely house. And it made me happy because you play piano for us. We was smiling smiling and I was very happy to see your lovely grass. And I was very happy I was very glad to see your garden the flowers are very good your tea was much better it was very good and so I enjoy more and more.
The end.

I should have known. What child doesn't need the grass and the trees? Lissa and Mandy are amongst the fortunate ones, they have acres of grass and thickets of trees and an assortment of pets wandering amongst them that would gladden the heart of any young person. *Rafiki ya Watoto* Kamau calls them, the children's friends.

*

They include, these friends of the children, two dogs, three cats, a budgerigar, a donkey, rabbits and a bush baby; we were also offered a baby elephant once but it died before we could accept.

The pets need time and attention which the girls cannot give them when they are at school. The staff are disinterested; love of animals is as much a social convention as polygamy or monogamy. Small children are instinctively cruel to living things and the Africans, when first the white man arrived here, were as surprised at his treatment of a useless cat (a dog at least kept guard over the house) as they were at his impatience with a child or neglect of an aged parent. They were resentful too – it is hardly surprising – when sometimes, in a European household, the animal received better treatment than they did themselves. The staff, then, cannot be expected to keep a lonesome donkey company, or tolerate a gregarious bush baby hopping up their legs or sitting on their heads.

As usual, when extra assistance is needed, or when something has to be fixed, sewn or repaired, Nan offers her services.

Energetic and spare – (although she will turn sideways in front of a mirror, point to a curve slighter than a crescent moon and insist that she is getting fat – she has black hair and lively blue eyes. Her face is thin and in its prominent bone formation and the resolute set of her lips, you can see at a glance the independence and the stubbornness that are as much a part of her Scottish ancestry as her stoicism and her loyalty. Shy and reserved, she has infinite patience and a great sense of humour – within the strict confines of the immediate family (outsiders would be astonished) she frequently acts the comic herself. She is particularly deft with a crochet hook and a knitting needle and has phenomenal success with jig-saw puzzles, fuses, Yorkshire pudding, children and, fortunately, animals.

She crossed the border into my parents' home when I was in my teens and she only in her twenties herself; it was shortly after Amanda was born, fourteen years ago, that she first set foot in Africa. It must have been the last place she dreamt of going to; Belgium was as far from home as she had ever been.

CIRCLE I

But she has an adventurous spirit and if she was ever homesick, which at the beginning I know she was, she was far too stoic ever to complain. She has her shortcomings like anyone else, but she derives her happiness from doing things for others; nothing is too much trouble, no pains too great.

She should have had children of her own, and she should have had six. But fate decreed differently, and Lissa and Mandy have been the beneficiaries of her devoted attention. She felt it as much as Monty and myself when first Lissa, then Mandy (albeit for one short term) went off to boarding-school. It was not through choice; I am totally against the British custom of sending their children to boarding-school from the age of six upwards. It seems obvious that an institution cannot provide the love and the bonds of normal family life, nor the freedom to express one's individuality, and it is disturbing to think of the calibre of some of the people to whom we so carelessly entrust our children. How many parents, I wonder, would be willing to admit that the staff of a school have more to give their children than they have themselves; nor, if the parents are intelligent, does a school have as much to offer in the *broader* sense of education. A good teacher is a rare and precious thing. Boarding-school is simply a social habit which is unthinkingly accepted like so many other customs, or used as a convenience, or in a firm belief in the necessity of its discipline. But in life it is not imposed discipline that is of importance, it is *self*-discipline, and the ability to accept responsibility.

Lissa's school in Kenya was a typical Dickensian anachronism (plenty of them still exist) with obsolete rules and draughty corridors and a narrow-minded outlook that was focused on discipline; happiness and mental stimulation were not included in the curriculum. Mandy was so unhappy there, when two years later she followed in her sister's footsteps, she ran away; my only regret is Lissa did not run with her. We sent her to the only day school, of the two or three that exist, that had room for her. Its academic reputation was not of the highest, but a sympathetic headmistress was energetically battling with this.

There are a majority of Africans at this school, a minority of Europeans, and Indians swell the ranks in between. It fascinates me to watch these girls pouring out of the building: every shape, size, shade, and denomination; Hindu, Muslim, Sikh, Kikuyu, Catholic, Protestant, Jew. And I find myself wondering why it is that aeroplanes are made faster, dresses shorter, blocks of offices and flats taller, yet the shape of education in so many schools remains basically the same. Poor girls, the same old learning by rote, the same old futile swotting, the same old dusty facts they will never use and all around that same old static building, the wonderful, miraculous world!

Lissa and Mandy, like so many other children, have always resented the hours of homework that have prevented them spending more time in the world of the garden with its chameleons and its cicadas, miniature tree frogs and stick insects, its fruits and its coffee, its opulent cactus flowers and its many birds: golden weavers, paradise fly-catchers, tufted bulbuls and hadada ibis that fly above the house with plaintive cries each morning before dropping down on to the grass to feed. Bees swarm in the roof and swallows have nested in the eaves; every so often a baby falls out of its nest and the girls try to save it (although never successfully) by putting it in a warmly lined box and dripping milk into its mouth every hour from a syringe. But it is, of course, the domestic animals that figure most importantly in their lives.

CIRCLE I

The smallest and most lively of these is Mitzy, the bush baby. When first we gave him to Lissa six years ago, he seemed only happy when she was carrying him around in the confined space, the darkness and the warmth of her shirt. He liked this so much that after a while he began to chatter angrily when she took him out, the first sign that his confidence was growing and his fear diminishing. He liked to nestle in her hair too, but for those first three weeks he never left her of his own volition; if she put him on a chair or a table he remained immobile as the furniture itself, waiting with a mute plea in his huge eyes to be returned to the safety of her body.

Quite suddenly, all this changed. One day he leapt across the carpet as though he had been shot out of a rocket, hopped on to the back of a chair and with a single jump sprang on top of the pelmet. From that moment on he was as active as before he had been static. He moves with such incredible speed, agility and accuracy – I don't think I have ever seen him knock anything over or miss his footing – that we have never grown tired of watching him. He urinates on his tiny hands before he leaps, probably to help him grip and also perhaps to mark the territory as his. If there is a picture or a beam for him to grasp, he can even land flat against the wall. Lissa put him on the kitchen scales once and the hand barely tipped four ounces. He has gained weight since then; perhaps it would now tip five. Stretched out, he is little more than twelve inches so that he is able to jump well over six times his own measurements in height, and almost as far in length. His long, furry tail probably helps his balance, while his acute hearing, his sharp eyesight and his speed are the only protection he has. His coat is soft as a swansdown powder-puff and his teeth, although as hurtful as a strong jab from a sewing needle, can do no more harm.

Bush babies are nocturnal and all day long Mitzy sleeps in his little wooden box which he likes to cram full of torn up face tissues and cotton wool. He wakens around six and Lissa takes him a tiny bowl of Farex and milk; for dessert he may fancy half a glacé cherry, a nibble of paw-paw or a taste of coconut. Marshmallow and chocolate he never refuses. He is also very fond of alcohol and they say that to catch a bush baby the Africans put *pombe* at the foot of a tree; later, when the bush babies have drunk their fill, the men shake the trees and the sleepy, drunken little creatures fall out. . . .

Mitzy has shared many a visitor's glass of whisky. Standing on his long hind legs he clutches the rim of the glass with delicate fingers (he is a primate) and drinks. His favourite dish is a live grasshopper or moth. Lissa catches them for him – preferably when Mandy isn't standing by making her feel like a murderess by murmuring oohs and ahs of pity for the captive prey – and hands them to him. He snatches the delicacy with a tiny hand and crunches into it with relish. When it rains and the flying ants swarm, a vibrant buzzing and a mist of lacey wings herald a banquet for Mitzy.

He used to keep us company at dinner, hopping across the table, nibbling at a piece of fruit or perching on someone's shoulder or foot. It was always hazardous though, for the servant sometimes forgot to close the door when he entered with a tray of food, and outside in the hall lurked a cat or a dog or both. Nor does Mitzy come when he's called. Perhaps it is because he has not forgiven us for making a fundamental mistake and giving him a girl's name – but then *everything* about a bush baby is so small!

His heedlessness almost cost him his life. One day he leapt out of Lissa's hand – and into the Alsatian's mouth. Lissa's

CIRCLE I

screams were blood curdling; we all leapt up from the table with an alacrity that might have matched Mitzy's own, and found her in the hall on her knees in an attitude of wild despair. Meantime, Honey dashed outside and into the coffee – with Mitzy still in her mouth. She had raced away in this fashion before, with a small poodle pup in her mouth, and once with a fluffy white rabbit – offspring of what we had deemed to be two males but apparently another of our fundamental errors.... Neither puppy nor rabbit were harmed. But how the frail and tiny Mitzy escaped with his life, and bounded from Honey's jaws on to the top of a coffee tree, is explicable only in terms of Jonah's escape from the whale.

There was a time when we toyed with the idea of releasing Mitzy. Two bush babies belonging to friends of ours had escaped from a tent. For thirty-six hours they were missing, but towards nightfall they appeared for their evening meal. Every night after that, a pattering of little feet on the canvas of the tent would signal their return. Far more sophisticated than Mitzy, they were eventually to travel half way round the world in an airline bag. One of them was to fall eight floors from a hotel window without hurting himself, and both were to frighten chambermaids from Paris to New York half out of their wits. (Help, help, there's a monkey in the room! *Au secours, au secours, il y a un grand RAT dans la chambre!*) But back in Kenya one of them was eventually taken by an owl; it was this that decided Mitzy's fate.

Although he no longer keeps us company during dinner, the girls often take Mitzy up to their room where he sometimes spends the night. He usually wakens them at intervals by hopping on to their faces; around day-break one of them lifts up the blankets and he shoots down to the bottom of the bed by their feet. There he lies sleeping till they waken him to put him in his little box. He is very irate at being thus disturbed and might stab a finger with a needle-like tooth if they do not handle him carefully. Once in his box he fusses with bits of cotton wool and tissues until he is comfortably ensconced and concealed from sight.

We often heard him calling, a small, high, oft-repeated note and thinking he was lonely, finally decided to try and find him a mate. Only a short while ago, we succeeded.

Mandy discovered a four-month-old female in the pet shop in Nairobi. For a day and a night, she kept the little animal with her. It was very nervous and sometimes bit her with its sharp little teeth in its fear — no one in the pet shop had handled it and it was quite unfamiliar with human beings. Finally, with some misgivings as we had no idea how Mitzy would react to this stranger infringing on his territory, Mandy went into the run to present Mitzy with his mate.

He flew at the little female in seeming fury, and she clawed back in terror. Mandy somehow managed to separate the two of them, her hands a mass of scratches, and tiny bites like perforations from fierce needles. That night she kept Mitzy in her room and left the newcomer in his run. We hoped that when Mitzy returned to the run, the female smell would be familiar to him and not take him by surprise, and that the intruder would have established some sort of right to his territory.

Once again, Mandy braved the introduction. This time Mitzy's behaviour was less aggressive and rather interesting. The female was curled up inside the little basket in which Mandy had brought it from Nairobi, and the lid was on –

deliberately: it seemed wiser to take things in easy stages, first to establish the female's presence in the run, second to release it....

But Mitzy leapt straight across to the basket – and knocked it over as he stood on his hind legs to peer inside. As it fell on its side on the wooden shelf where Mitzy's little box stands, the lid came off. We all held our breaths and watched. Mitzy darted inside, and stood over the little female, concealing her completely, holding her prisoner as it were, but not harming her. And there he stayed. After some time, he peered out over the edge of the basket – then returned to his stance over the body of the cowering female.

Later that day, his predominance presumably indisputably established, he gave her her freedom and seemed to accept her completely. Perhaps one of these days we will find three bush babies in the run; nothing could be more wondrously minute than a baby bush baby.

Apart from disappearances into vases, drawers, coat pockets, pipes leading from basins, where he once spent several hours while we distractedly turned the house upside-down hunting for him, Mitzy is the smallest of and the least troublesome of the girls' pets.

Wambo was the largest and the most problematical. She was one of a wild herd, a little Catalonian foal lassoed on a ranch some hundred miles away and brought to her new home kicking and struggling in the back of a Land-Rover. We had not thought to go so far afield but none of the Africans nearby seemed willing to part with their donkeys, valuing their working potential more than the money. Amanda had been yearning for this foal for what seemed to her in the timelessness of childhood an infinity of months, so that when one day she came home and found Wambo waiting for her, she approached the animal with the dream-like expression of a sleep-walker.

Humans were destined to remain Wambo's friends. Tito, the Ridgeback, growing old now, was irascible with her, and Honey insane with jealousy. She would make lightning attacks on the foal, pulling lumps of fur from her neck or flank. Eventually a day came when Wambo flew back at her, and now began a crazy game in which the two animals would chase after one another partly in hostility, partly in play. The garden was transformed into a frenzied arena then, with Wambo's hoofs pounding against the earth as she tore past the house. Her boldness increased and now she began to chase the girls across the grass too – sometimes followed by the dogs, and even the cats, in a wild cortège. As she gained on the girls the excitement grew, for they never knew whether she would stop – or charge into them full pelt. If they dashed for the nearest tree she would career round it in ever decreasing circles, stop within a yard of them, buck joyously and race off again.

At first we had had problems feeding her. She disliked the rubber teat and had had to learn to suck milk from a bowl. Gradually her tastes broadened until she was eating everything from the dining-room curtains to Lissa's hair and ice cream, for which she had a consuming passion. When we lunched outside, the uninvited guest with the flamboyant manners would stroll into the summerhouse and stand with her head over the table, blink her beautiful eyes, and calmly demolish everything edible within sight. There was a time when I thought the equine species was herbivorous; I am now much wiser.

When we dined inside, she would skip up the six steep steps on to the dining-room veranda and stand half inside the french windows, half out, deterred only by the slipperiness of the wooden floor from entering completely, and wait patiently for the girls to join her. She expected to join in all their activities now.

But a crisis was pending. The garden is Monty's forte. He has broken, planted and terraced it; he has fought with Kamau's stubbornness and my own horticultural inadequacy. Now Wambo threatened to lay waste every flower-bed, chew the blossoms off every bush and the creepers off every wall. I felt for Monty, and I too found it distressing.

At the same time it seemed to me unthinkable to give a child a pet, allow her to grow to love it, then take it away.

Often, if you have the patience and the restraint to leave things alone, they have a way of working themselves out. Unlike Monty, I am deficient in both these qualities, but this time waiting was the only hope. And so the matter was dropped and allowed to drift.

Soon the rains came and with them, the new grass that Monty had planted on the other side of the garden near the banana trees. Tempted by the succulent shoots, Wambo wandered away from the house – and at the same time, the anthureum lilies, the orange clivea and the purple patrea. The problem, it seemed, was solved. In any case, by this time she had pressed her entrée into the household with such character and verve there was no longer any question of her withdrawal.

One day I came home and found the house strangely quiet. It was the weekend. I had left the girls making batiks (watched by an admiring Lucy), and Monty clipping tumbling sprays of bougainvillaea. The only proof on my return that I had not dreamt all this was the strong smell of wax from the batiks wafting through the house.

Eventually I found everyone in the paddock with Wambo. She had developed a sudden attack of colic and was already too weak to stand. We even had to lift her head out of the grass so that she could breathe.

The next day, though neither Monty nor I had expected her to live through the night, she was standing on her feet, and the day after she had regained sufficient strength to walk around the garden and nibble a little grass. In her coltish prettiness she seemed very much part of the spring-like sunshine and the new shoots of bamboo. That afternoon she lay down in the sun as she often did outside the kitchen door, and towards dark the girls took her back to the paddock for the night. Later that evening they went to give her the rest of the medicine prescribed by the vet.

I was up in my room and I heard a strange sound in the garden – an animal in pain perhaps? The sound grew nearer and I knew then that it was the children crying. I knew as well that Wambo was dead.

The grief of a small child is unbearable, there are no words to fill the gap left by death and it is no good trying to rationalize or philosophize. The night had a hollowness to it, the death of a little donkey and the grief of two small girls carved an empty place in the house.

In the morning the swallows emerged from their nests beneath the eaves of the house, sat upon the window-sills and lustily heralded the morning. Mitzy, exhausted from a night's capers, retired into his little box to sleep away the daylight hours; Kamau leisurely raked leaves, splay feet bare and clothed in tatters, and Lucy waited by the swamp for her daily lift to school. Soon, a new, eager pup was rushing behind the girls across the lawn as Amanda was too heartbroken to consider another donkey, and life, in time, replenished and overflowed the hollow place, as it always does.

CIRCLE II

Peter's Camp, the Ngong Hills and the Masai Wells

A LITTLE further from home, in the Ngong Hills, the old world is shared by the Masai and the game. One still meets a warrior striding across the slopes, there are still herds of buffalo, magnificent eland and shy waterbuck. Nearer to home still – only three or four miles the other side of the city in fact – lies Nairobi Game Park.

A park, in this country, is not a fenced piece of land. It may be thousands of square acres, but the animals that roam across them are protected. They are only protected from man. It is not necessary to protect them from each other because with the possible exception of the leopard, animals kill only for food, meticulously retaining nature's balance in the process. It is ironical that in this age of scientific advance it is only we human beings who are unable to do this, yet at the same time we alone have the power to interfere with nature's checks and balances. It is ironical that man can – and does – control the number of animals, but so far he has found no solution to his own population explosion. And until he does, the game will continue to recede and diminish until one day it disappears from the face of the earth. It is frightening that so much which comes under the label of progress leads to the destruction of nature and of beauty. I think this is the underlying feeling of wonder, and even relief, visitors experience when they find wild animals in their natural habitat so near to a busy little city. It is for this reason too that the Ngong Hills have a special significance. They are twenty miles from the house, and although the nearest approach is from the north, sometimes we take the more rugged entrance from the south, passing Peter Beard's camp *en route*. It lies between the Game Park and the Hills, giraffe wander through the bushes, a leopard lurks in the vicinity and recently four lions invaded the premises, refusing to leave until two days later they were chased away with thunder flashes. As for the wart-hogs, encouraged by their daily meal of maize, they have almost taken over and wander familiarly amongst the tents.

The tents are protected by sloping eaves of thatch and each one has a wooden floor like a low platform; this makes them seem very permanent abodes indeed, which doubtless they will be for Peter prefers tents to houses. The canvas sides of the 'living-room' are adorned with Arabian daggers, trinkets from Zanzibar and one or two of Peter's own paintings and photographs. The two tables are littered with an assortment of intriguing objects: monstrous Indian carvings, bizarre skeletons and skulls, weird pebbles from Lake Rudolf, heavy silver from Lamu, a hideous frog with a mobile scarlet tongue, a painting by Peter's idol and guru, Picasso, side by side with a meek and pious picture of Krishna. . . .

Each of the objects on the table is symbolic of Peter's character and the extremes which make it up: his passion for the genuine and his scorn of the banal, his attraction to the violent and the bizarre and his dedication to an ideal or to art, his curiosity and his creativity, his energy and his destructivity. Each one of us is a combination of opposites to a greater or a lesser degree; with Peter, it is to the greatest degree. This is half his individuality, half the vividness of his personality which either wins people to him completely so that they will go to any lengths for him – or turns them headlong in the opposite direction. Just as Peter is all praise or all vitriolic, all love or all hate, all despondency – or more characteristically – all enthusiasm, so people are totally for or against him. Essentially gregarious and yet at the same time the original loner, every now and then Peter takes off into the bush for a month or two, or to his favourite haunts on the wild shores of Lake Rudolf. His only luggage then is his bedroll, a jar each of mayonnaise and peanut butter, and several boxes of Ritz crackers; he travels light as the nomads, and with his physical strength and his stamina, has something of their powers of endurance.

Thirteen years ago, as a youth of seventeen, he read Karen Blixen's (or Isak Dinesen's) *Out of Africa*. It so stirred his imagination he was compelled to visit the land described in the book with such poignant perceptiveness. He came, he saw and he was conquered. It is not by chance that his camp faces on to Karen Blixen's beloved Ngong Hills, or that her servant Kamante now works for him. Nor is it merely coincidence that his own book *The End of the Game* should start with the title 'The Africa of Isak Dinesen', for he has diverted a part of his energy and his determination into researching the life and work of this woman.

A talented photographer and a writer, Peter is primarily an artist. Totally unconventional in many ways (though he may exchange shorts and a sports shirt for a sports jacket and trousers in extreme circumstances, or even go so far as to wear socks with his sandals), he yet returns periodically to the folds of the Emily Post New York society against which he rebelled. I wonder how they receive the unprodigal son with his boyish grin and lively, intent eyes. A person of dogmatic views and a tendency to express them in colourful diatribes rather than mere logic, arguments swarm round Peter like bees smoked from a hive. And through all the activity and bluster of his life, with something of the cool quietness and a little of the uncertainty of a lunar presence, glides the dark-eyed, flowing-haired Minnie, his beautiful wife.

It was a far cry from a sophisticated life in Manhattan to the camp overlooking the Ngong Hills where, by night, a giraffe drifted from the shadows into the moonlight and, by day, a pet goat and a donkey fraternized with the wart-hogs – soon to be joined by an uninvited one-eyed vervet monkey. There were also two bush babies; the same that were to journey in a travel bag half around the world.

The one-eyed monkey used to de-flea the bush babies, comfortably ensconced on Minnie and Peter's bed. The monkey was a great favourite with the girls, but I disliked him intensely. His playfulness was subject to fits of irrational fury which so frightened me that, although no one else seemed to mind, I began to visit the camp with growing reluctance. Then one day, despite all the affection she lavished on him, Northey-Chongo flew at Mandy, savagely clawing and scratching her arm. I think his treacherousness hurt her as much as the physical pain, for no one had been more attached to him or played with him more delightedly. Northey-Chongo attacked her a second time. Undeterred, she continued to pamper and play with him; after the third attack, she began to share my reluctance to visit the camp.

One day, irritated by his impudence perhaps, as he searched for fleas in their coats or gambolled amongst them as they fed,

An early morning stroll in the garden after feeding Wambo

Mandy and the unpredictable Northey Chongo

Mitzy's only defence is his agility and his speed

A Masai boy on the wide, windswept slopes between the Ngong Hills and the Masai wells

Dusk at Naivasha

Masai women intrigued by Lissa's and Mandy's hair

one of the wart-hogs gored Northey-Chongo and brought about his death. They gored the donkey, too, and Kamante neatly stitched the wound and bandaged it. Karen Blixen had taught him on the farm, he reminded us when Lissa and I arrived at the camp the day after the accident; she had taught him to stitch humans too.

For some time now, Peter and Minnie have been away in the States and every so often the girls and I drop by at the camp. You cannot lock tents and Peter, with an unconcern for his possessions equal to his disregard of personal danger, leaves his domain with the trust of a priest and the light-hearted irresponsibility of a gipsy.

Kamante comes to meet us when we arrive, a stout stick in his hand to ward off the wart-hogs now that they have grown so bold. Frequently they start to fight, and then the camp is turned into a circus, wart-hogs racing in all directions. They quickly settle down again as a wart-hog's appetite far outweighs his pugnacity. Bending their forelegs they grovel in the earth and scoff the grain with few manners and no grace. Satiated at last, they wander away to welter in the mud wallow Peter has made for them, followed by Wilhelmina, the goat. The moment they depart, a flock of tiny birds waiting in a nearby tree drop down like a sudden shower of rain to peck at the remaining grains of maize.

We leave Kamante and go into the studio. A soft brightness filters through the skylight like sunshine through layers of gauze. The studio roof creaks in the wind, and the branches of the old tree that grows straight through it, sway. Outside, in the thick bush that makes a secret place of the studio, birds sing and leaves mutter and whisper. A shaft of sunlight spills through the door and on to the floor; Kamante is standing there, a gaunt old man now with white hair. I look through the precious collection of Africana on the wide white shelves until I come to *Out of Africa*; taking it down I turn to the chapter on Kamante to refresh my memory. The magic of the pages draws me again, involuntarily I sit down and read on:

Kamante when I first met him looked as if he were six years old, but he had a brother who looked about eight and both brothers agreed that Kamante was the eldest of them, so I suppose he must have been set back in growth by his long illness; he was probably then nine years old. He grew up now, but he always made the impression of being a dwarf, or in some way deformed, although you could not put your finger on the precise spot that made him look so. His angular face was rounded with time ... (but) his legs remained forever as thin as sticks. A fantastic figure he always was, half of fun and half of diabolism; with a very slight alteration, he might have sat and stared down, on the top of the Cathedral of Nôtre Dame in Paris. He had in him something bright and alive; in a painting he would have made a spot of unusually intense colouring; with this he gave a stroke of picturesqueness to my household. He was never quite right in the head, or at least he was always what, in a white person, you would have called highly eccentric.... He was all his life in his own way an isolated figure....

Outside, the hills are waiting. They flow like folds of velvet and the moss-green slopes are awash with shadows from brimming hollows and drifts of clouds. The Kikuyu say that one day God buried a good man and as he lifted his hand and let the soil slip through his fingers, it settled into the four peaks of the Ngong Hills. Approaching from the southern end, several miles past Peter's camp the path that leads in to the range is narrow and winding, pitted with hollows and scarred with rocks. The thick bushes on either side seem reluctant to allow it to pass but it escapes their hold, shoots suddenly

CIRCLE II

skywards, then plunges down again. Free now, it flows across the steep, grassy slopes, home of buffalo and antelopes and a few rhino. Way below, the vast lick of plain curls lazily round rocky hills the colour of burnt corn, sand and honey, African colours, arid and tawny. Feet in the green grass, head in the strong breeze, one looks down upon a limitless, burnt view. Here is the beginning of the real Africa; here too begins the territory of the Masai.

*

The land where the Masai roam extends beyond the Ngong Hills in one direction, and across the Great Rift Valley, past Lake Naivasha, in the other. The Great Rift Valley, at a certain juncture, drops away beneath a sheer escarpment edged by a steeply winding road. It unfurls itself like a vast brown hammock, its far side battened to the sky, its far end entwined at some infinite point with the horizon. It stretches all the way from the Jordan Valley to southern Tanzania and Mozambique, a huge depression in the earth pitted with lakes and tumescent with extinct volcanoes – Longanot, Suswa and Elementaita amongst them.

Naivasha, haunt of dozens of varieties of birds, is the nearest lake to home. Pelicans skim the surface like old-fashioned aquaplanes, greater grebes stand amongst the water-lilies by the shore and herons nest in the secret isles of papyrus. The other side of the water are low hills and at dusk, when the fish eagles call their wild, lone farewells, the lake mirrors the silver gleam of the sky; its beauty at this hour is hauntingly tranquil.

Large ranches run down to the water's edge. Zebra and eland and gazelles and the occasional elephant, share the grassland with fine, hump-backed Boran cattle and a few imported herds that must make the heart of a Masai beat with furious desire.

An extinct volcano overlooks the lake, its fissured sides rising steeply into a circular rim. It is called *Longanot*, Masai for fissured; the Masai love words and they have given each of their mountains and lakes several names. Kilimanjaro they call Great Hill, or *Donyo Ebor*, White Mountain, and they call it too House of God, for their God dwells upon its summit just as the God of the Kikuyu dwells upon Kerinyaga. They are great orators and the famous speeches of their leaders have been handed down from generation to generation by word of mouth. One of these was made by the great prophet-chief Batian, about a hundred years ago:

When our father Batian was about to die, (a Masai warrior relates) he called together all the elders and the warriors of the Masai. We came in great numbers, until the place was black with us, even as our villages are black with flies in the time of the rains. We sat round in lines, curved like the moon when she is first born, and our father Batian sat amongst us in full sight and hearing of us all. . . . Then he rose and pointing to the great hills he spoke: 'I see no men: all are finished and gone down.' He sat down again, and covered his eyes with his hands, we were all sitting silent, for the breath had gone from us. Again he looked where he alone saw, and said: 'Now I see neither men nor cattle, the cattle have followed my children and the land is empty and bare as the palm of my hand is empty and bare.' But after a long silence he spoke again, seeing further into the future and giving them words of hope. 'They are coming, they are coming those who will protect and save my children. See you them not, first one, then many, many until the land is full of them, and peace and plenty again reign. See you not the man, who is not a man, but a god, with a fair and shining white face, and behind him many more, until my eyes cannot see the end of them all, all fair and white.

CIRCLE II

These god-men will follow quickly on evil times, they will live on my land and they will care for my children when I shall be no more. My eyes shall never see them; fear them not for they will protect you.'*

A generation or two after Batian had made this speech, a vicious outbreak of smallpox wiped out a large proportion of the tribe ('I see no men: all are finished and gone down'), and an equally vicious outbreak of rinderpest wiped out a large proportion of their cattle ('Now I see neither men nor cattle, the cattle have followed my children and the land is empty'). The Kikuyu were now dominant and the arrival of the man with the 'fair and shining face' was opportune, for they protected Batian's children, as he foretold, from the Kikuyu; at the same time, however, these 'god-men' that 'followed quickly on evil times' also pushed the Masai back out of some of their most fertile territory, occupied it themselves and called it the 'White Highlands'.

But vast tracks of land, much of it fertile, all of it fair to look upon, were reserved for the Masai, and this land is occupied by them still.

In the opposite direction to Lake Naivasha from the house, some thirty miles beyond the Ngong Hills, there is a place where many Masai gather at midday to water their cattle at a series of wells. The wells are little known – which is hardly surprising considering how difficult it is to find them. The route is particularly beautiful, the stoney track leading past green and windswept slopes below which the plain flows freely outwards till it is finally curbed by hills and mountains.

The Last of the Masai by Sidney and Hildegarde Langford Hinde, published by William Heinemann Ltd, 1901.

When the road suddenly begins to descend, the bush closes in and it grows quickly hotter. At a certain point, an almost imperceptible track leads off into the bush itself; it is so narrow the safari car seems to push its way through the branches like a thick thread through the eye of a thin needle. There are tall cacti and craggy rock formations, and it is difficult to believe that we were high in the cool hills only twenty miles back. After a while, the path peters out and trees and rocks make it impossible to drive any further. At this point even Monty, who has an almost infallible sense of direction, has to think which way to turn.

Last time we went to the wells, two Masai warriors accompanied us on the last lap of the safari. They were carrying spears and knobkerries, and their hair, threaded with thin strips of leather and caked with ochre and cattle fat, hung down the back of their necks in a thick coil. I remembered my first encounter with Masai: how they had halted us by standing in the middle of the path, spears raised, and clambered aboard the vehicle, grinning and grunting with pleasure as it gathered a little speed; how thrilled and utterly incredulous I had felt to find myself beside real live warriors who until that moment had existed for me only in the pages of a geography book. White people were still a novelty to them and they were intrigued by us as well – my hair especially (they were unable, in the end, to keep their hands off it), and our portable radio. They had pressed their ears close to it and tried to imitate it, then spontaneously begun to dance, leaping high into the air with their extraordinary agility, their plaited hair flying. But it was our medicine and ointments they valued most of all and each day they would bring a patient for treatment.

Whatever else may fail to impress the Masai in the white

man's way of life, respect for our white witch-doctors at least prevails. And the two warriors who were taking us to the wells requested us first to help a sick man.

They took us to some huts and outside one of them a youth lay unconscious. The Kikuyu believe that if a man dies in his hut, his spirit will haunt it and they burn it down. This perplexes me because the presence of such spirits in the family land is of such importance, a Kikuyu of traditional beliefs would not leave it for fear of the consequences that would befall him. A Masai, I once read, believes that for an ordinary mortal, death is final; the spirit of a rich man or a witch-doctor however turns into a snake (which is interesting because occasionally there is a mythological affinity between hero and snake), while that of a great chief goes to heaven. 'Heaven' I am sure, is a loose interpretation of the word, especially as traditional African belief does not include the concept of heaven and hell. The Masai must mean the sky, and space; where else would one expect a great nomadic spirit to go?

The sick youth's eyelids fluttered. He seemed a long way from either extinction, snakes or the sky, and we promised to take him to hospital on our way home.

We walked on through the bushes with the two warriors. It was mid-afternoon, it was hot and it was dusty, but it was good to feel the atmosphere of the bush again. Soon we came to a collection of hillocks – formed no doubt by the earth that was originally excavated from the wells. The wells themselves look like sunken miniature canals, a small maze of them. The Masai had told us when first we visited this spot that they themselves, of course, had not excavated the wells but hired another tribe to do so, just as they had always hired the Wanderobo to make and paint their shields for them, paying by a system of barter.

They had also told us that each herdsman was allocated a certain well and despite the number of them and their maze like arrangement, each animal went unerringly to its own watering place.

A few Masai collected round us, their eyes constantly straying to the girls' hair which always fascinates them by its length and colour and texture, A young warrior stuck his spear into the ground and leant against it; a calf descended the steep bank of a well, stood in the water and drank. The sun beat down, it was very still, and there was the old, slow pulse beat of that other world. . . .

Beyond the turn-off to the wells, the road continues its descent until it arrives, finally, at the low hot regions of Lake Magadi. This salt and soda lake looks more like desolate snow fields, and a few isolated mountains are grouped intermittently round it. There are pelicans and flamingoes and many other birds, yet I do not recall hearing any birds singing on the two occasions I have been to the lake, it has always been strangely silent and still – dead almost. Because (I assume) it has been a Sunday or a holiday, even the bizarre factory, whose appearance reminds me of a monstrous semi-ruined barn with op art trimmings, looked utterly abandoned. A gravel path raised two or three feet above the salt and soda encrusted water leads across the lake and beyond this, perhaps another forty miles or so, lies the most beautiful part of the land roamed by the Masai.

Until very recently there was no road to the Nguramen Escarpment. Then Philip Leakey, youngest son of the anthropologist Louis Leakey, came to know this area on foot; he managed to obtain a lease on it from the Masai and undertook the arduous task of making a path to the Nguramen – where he is now building a game lodge.

CIRCLE II

He is very possessive about this untouched part of Kenya, and he calls it *'nchi ya* Leakey', Leakey's land. Tall, gangling, his dreamy blue eyes and fair hair combine to give a delicate impression more indicative of his feelings for the incredible beauty of this part of the land than a certain wildness and the tough and active life he leads. Apart from building a lodge and making a road, he takes people on walking safaris, engaging columns of porters to carry the loads just as the explorers did in the early days. Several years younger than Peter Beard – he is twenty-four or five – Philip reminds me of Peter in some ways. Both are loners and individualists; both enjoy a tough, active life in the bush; neither pays much attention to the conventions and neither takes well to organization nor, despite what they manage to accomplish, leads a particularly organized life.

The lodge that Philip will soon have completed is situated by a stream, in amongst the trees. But he also has a tented camp in the forest on the mountain. To reach this you drive up the Nguramen Escarpment, the vehicle jolting and shaking, one moment nosing skywards the next diving towards the earth, until eventually you come to a plateau. One side of this plateau is a ravine, behind it a steep cliff face whose towering rocks are covered in ancient forest; on the other side there is a vast view across the hills to some distant spot where, on a fine day, you can see both Kerinyaga and Kilimanjaro. Soon after this you enter a forest where the path that Philip has made eventually runs out. Then you leave your vehicle and walk.

There are no Masai in this part of their land and no cattle, for there is tsetse fly. But for some strange reason the flies only seem to bother you when you are in a moving vehicle and never once when we were walking did we see a single one. The escarpment, the plateau, the forest, the mountain and all the surrounding land are virtually untouched, no vehicles have traversed them, there are no people, and Philip's habitations (which he is careful to keep completely concealed in the trees) are the first.

The forest is full of game and birds. There are secret pools ringed by tall trees and coming suddenly upon one of these we startled a saddle-billed stork standing in the shallow water. With a flash of vivid carmine and a span of great grey wings the bird rose through the primordial stillness like some mythological creature on the day of creation.

We stayed the night in the forest and in the morning Philip took us to a point on the edge of the plateau from which we gazed down at one of those views that make you catch your breath – then forget everything else.

Running down a grassy slope and clambering between slabs of sandy-pink rocks typical of the area, we found ourselves standing on the edge of the plateau. The wind blew keen and strong, bowing the feathered heads of the tall grass; behind us, on the other side of the plateau, the forest-clad cliff face of the Loita Hills towered to meet the sky. It was clouded, so that the land way below us was completely unadorned – no draperies of golden light, no dark folds of shadow, only the great clusters of hills directly beneath us were definitely coloured, green still from the recent rain. Then the earth simply hurled itself out with a sort of huge, implacable wildness, enfolding Kilimanjaro and Kerinyaga in its embrace, and flowing onwards to some infinite point where one could no longer distinguish it from the sky. To the East lay Lake Natron in Tanzania, its thirty mile stretch of water flanked at intervals by isolated mountains named by the Masai, Ol Donyo Sambu, Shombole (both still in Kenya), Ol Donyo Lengai and Ngorongoro. Apart from

CIRCLE II

Ol Donyo Sambu, its head a massive slab of rock sloping dramatically skywards rather like the open lid of a gigantic grand piano, it is not the shapes or the colours that I remember most vividly when I recall this particular view; it is a mysterious quality like the background of a pre-Renaissance painting – the mystery of the unknown (which perhaps corresponds to the unknown spheres of man's mind and may be partly the reason why such a view moves us so), the hazy intimation of the beginning of things; for this is Africa as it always has been, and Kenya as the first Masai saw it.

En route to the Nguramen Escarpment we had come to a river that flowed slowly between deep earth banks. Many cattle were crossing, some swimming and some fording the water. A slim, naked Masai boy of some nine years old was poised on the far bank encouraging the cattle to cross; another boy clad in a sarong squatted in the middle of the dusty road watching us. The scene was compelling. Once again we were being drawn back in time; the movement of the herds, the flow of the water, the timelessness of the naked Masai boy, the cows caught in the dust-filtered sunlight as they emerged from the river and disappeared along the path. This too – like the view, like the forest – was Africa as it always was, and untold centuries are concentrated into such moments of direct confrontation with the past. It is, I believe, an integral part of the magnetism of Africa herself and of those of her people who, like the Masai, have remained unaffected by the changes we choose to label progress (despite the future predicted as a result of them), and who have retained a stronger link than we have done with nature and another time.

That the nomads of Kenya's North have remained unchanged is less surprising; their land is so inhospitable none has coveted it, and no foreign customs or ideas (other than those of the missionaries which, like the Masai, they have resisted) have been spread amongst its people. But the Masai, having pushed southwards in search of more fertile regions, saw the former stamping grounds of their cattle tilled and planted and witnessed the harvests of tea and coffee, of pyrethrum and wheat. They saw roads being built and houses of stone erected, they gazed upon cars and trains, machinery and aeroplanes, they knew of the white man's knowledge and they were aware of his manifold possessions, yet still they remained unimpressed and, desiring none of this, continued to live as in days of yore.

Their manner of living had – has – a strict structure to it, and it is a structure common to the majority of tribes in this country, agricultural as well as pastoral, although the customs and beliefs of each differs within it.

The first stage is, of course, birth followed by childhood, during which the son of a pastoralist learns to herd cattle and the son of an agriculturist learns to work the soil. Between the ages of approximately twelve and sixteen, whenever the elders decide to hold the ceremony for this age group, the boys and girls are circumcised and enter the third phase of their lives: man or womanhood.

I do not know if the accompanying responsibilities impressed upon a Kikuyu are impressed with the same stress and seriousness upon a Masai, although the ceremony itself is as important, as ritualistic and as elaborate. But the years that follow seem markedly carefree, for this is a time for love and a time for dancing, a time for talking and a time for singing, and the young people live apart from the rest of the clan – just as the Hippies in the West form their own colonies in their pathetic attempts, which meet with so little success, to achieve the same simple and joyous existence.

Unlike the Hippies, this period in the life of a Masai is preparatory for the next, and while he is enjoying himself he is preparing with the utmost seriousness to become a warrior. Traditionally, to prove himself he must kill a lion, after which he may grow his hair, dress it in ceremonial fashion and finally, to the accompaniment of another great ceremony, he receives his shield and his spear.

During this time a Masai *moran* may eat only meat and drink only milk, or milk mixed with blood; they are not permitted to partake of the vegetable paste prepared by the women, nor are they allowed any possessions. They practise hurling their spears, and learn the art of warfare. From childhood a Masai boy is assigned a place in juxtaposition to other warriors during warfare, and the pattern on his shield will designate both his rank and this position. If a warrior meets other men *en route* to battle, he knows exactly between which two men he must stand and this military formation is adhered to with strict disciplinary order. The Masai have a reputation for valour and fairness in war; they are said never to attack without warning, and never to run away. They are chivalrous too and one story tells how once they punished another tribe for permitting their women to be sold as slaves; another tells of a pact they once made with the Kikuyu whereby the women of both tribes were to go unharmed during the border clashes and raids. Although a Kikuyu will not marry a Masai girl, the Masai men, with their eye for a pretty woman, are not at all averse to a plump and prolific Kikuyu girl who, unlike her menfolk, will sometimes marry into this tribe. Not very long ago Mandy spent some time at a Masai *manyatta* where a few young Americans were making a documentary film. One of the women took her to one side and when the two of them were alone, told Amanda she would like her to marry her son, and that they would paint her with ochre so that she would not look so very different! To which I replied, when Mandy told me, that this was all very well, but Monty and I were asking a tremendously high bride price and I doubted whether the young man's father would have sufficient cattle to pay it!

Usually it is only when the phase of warriorship is over that a man may choose a wife and marry. Amongst the Kikuyu it was a terrible disgrace for a woman to fall pregnant before marriage and the man was severely punished. Traditionally, although it was common practice for a young girl to spend the night with a young man, she must wear her 'soft leather apron' between her thighs so that the closest possible physical contact was encouraged without allowing the sexual act. Nor would the youth remove the apron unless he knew the girl very well, for fear she might tell the rest of the age group who would then ostracize him.*

When a Masai is leaving warriorship behind him and stepping across the threshold into the phase of husband, his head is ceremonially shaved – only a *moran* is permitted the elaborate coiffeur. The heads of married women are also shaved and they wear numerous metal bracelets and anklets.

I had always wondered how they came by these metal ornaments because I knew that they possessed them before the advent of the white man and that they were of some significance in their lives. Then I discovered that the smiths (belonging to a

* *Facing Mount Kenya* by Jomo Kenyatta, published by Secker & Warburg.

tribe called the Il-Kunono) take sand or gravel from the river beds, mix it with clay, spread it on a skin on the floor of a furnace, then blast the furnace with bellows for four days. Only when they have feasted on a cow may the pig-iron be drawn out and hammered into shape.

Other tribes fear the smiths, for to them their art seems as magic. Even the Masai, who although they have their taboos are comparatively unsuperstitious, respect them and used to permit them to accompany them to war, bearing their swords and shields – the latter made for them by the Wanderobo. It is said that although the Masai treat the Il-Kunono and the Wanderobo almost as vassals, they always paid for their services meticulously in kind.

As a married man, the Masai is permitted such luxuries as an ivory snuff box and tobacco, and his diet, although monotonous and frugal to the extreme compared with our own, is no longer so restricted. Now he spends his time visiting his friends – a Masai can walk up to sixty miles in a day – and talking as only a Masai knows how to talk, round and round the point, drawing it out to its fullest, most flavoursome length.

Life for the older Masai woman is less hedonistic. It is she who must fetch water and wood and build huts. But as amongst most tribal people in this country, an old woman is accorded a position of great veneration, and it is through her, as the grandchildren gather round her for an evening to listen, that all the old myths and traditions are handed down. It is thanks to her that we know the first Masai was called Kideni, and that he was hairy, and that he stood on top of Mount Kilimanjaro and beat a mighty calabash and all the women came running. He made love to them, and caused them to fall pregnant, and thus begat the first Masai people who, the legend assures us, were not hairy at all.

Like the Kikuyu, the last stage of a man's life, if he has proved himself, is that of eldership and leader of the people. Birth, childhood, manhood, warriorhood, husband, father, elder; a steady progression, like the rungs in a ladder, towards a higher place in life and in society. So that old age is the summit of the hill and the time of harvest – and not as in our world, the ravaged valley.

I have long been aware of – and been intrigued by – the different conception of time an African has from our own. But I could not of course understand it. Then, just as I was completing this book, I came across John Mbiti's *African Religions and Philosophy** in which I discovered that the African traditional concept of time does not include the future. Time for them is comprised of events, and as events only exist after they have happened or while they are happening, the future, in which no events have yet taken place, has no meaning. This emphasis on the now (and the past out of which it has crystallized, or is crystallizing) rules out the Western preoccupation with a happier, more prosperous tomorrow – usually illusory – and is conducive to satisfaction in the present moment.

Dirt, disease, ignorance, all these are curable, yet despite our progress in medicine and science we have not yet managed to cure one of our own most prevalent ailments: our obsession with time; the desperate, frequently neurotic need to retain a youthful appearance, the crazy compulsion to arrive at destinations ever more quickly. One might object that we do a great deal more with our time than a Masai, but for the majority it is

* Published by Heinemann.

obligatory in order to exist (where in any case is all our activity taking us to?), and the motive is usually to obtain the one commodity the Masai already possess in abundance: a little leisure in which to relax.

A few years ago Monty had to try and persuade a number of Masai to take part in a film. In accordance with tradition the *baraza* was held beneath an enormous fig tree. It was very picturesque, for Kilimanjaro's gleaming white dome towered in the background and the slender limbs of the Masai reclining or sitting on the ground made symmetrical copper patterns in the green grass. The elders and Monty were gathered beneath the fig tree and each man, Monty included, held the traditional *rungu* in his hand when his turn came to speak. The people decided in favour: yes, they would permit a number of their men to appear in the film. Just then a car drew up and out stepped their M.P. Within thirty seconds he reversed the decision it had taken a couple of hours to make. He would not, he said, allow his people to display themselves as museum pieces.

Museum pieces – or Africa's heritage? For Africa has her own heritage and her own wisdom and it is fast becoming smothered beneath layers of other customs and other values in the way that old paintings in churches are sometimes smothered beneath centuries of plaster or paint.

Spear in hand, elaborately coiffeured, a warrior occasionally wanders along the shrub planted streets of Nairobi. The modern buildings, the busy traffic, impress him not one whit. If the wind blows his sarong and reveals his slim nudity, he is totally unashamed. Arrogantly indifferent to the tumultuous changes around him, confronting them with an equanimity which is born of the pride and freedom he has inherited from his forefathers and from that natural acceptance of life and death he has gleaned from his closeness to the earth, he prefers his own way of life – and is hanging on to it for as long as he can, a superb exclamation mark in the impressive annals of 'progress' and mechanization.

CIRCLE III

Into the Bush

JOLTING over rutted paths or ploughing our way through thick mud, our safaris cross the age-old paths of the elephant, take us through primaeval forest and over stone wastelands, past desolate lakes and migrating game, past Masai *manyattas* and nomad caravans, and the secret depths of volcanic craters. The mere sight of the loaded safari car and the little two-wheeler trailer packed ready for departure conjures up the smell of dust, the feel of stillness, and a foretaste of that freedom which is the birthright of the nomads. Stowed away into the small space of the vehicles is everything that we need to live; here is freedom of movement, freedom from the clock and freedom from conventions. Here too is completeness, because safari for us is essentially a family affair, the simplicity and fullness of life in the bush something that Lissa and Mandy, and Monty and I, enjoy equally and together.

We have camped on the banks of a rushing river and we have camped in a dried up river bed that wound like an eerie tunnel beneath tortuous branches; we have camped by quiet crater lakes and we have camped amongst thorn trees where the grass is scanty and dry as straw, where the wind blows strong and the sun is hot and there is not a particle of humidity in the pure clear air. Carmine bee-eaters, malachite kingfishers, paradise fly-catchers, golden weavers and lilac-breasted rollers have darted amongst the branches above our heads; iridescent starlings and red and white buffalo weavers have shared our breakfast. Of a morning we have found lions' spoor round the camp; by night we have listened to the screaming of baboons, the cry of bush babies and the sigh of the wind in the doum palms.

Every safari I have been on has its own special flavours and memories. At Samburu, where the border line divides Kenya's south from the desert and semi-desert of the north, I remember particularly elephant filing silently behind our tent in the moonlight and buffalo crossing the Ouasa Nyiro river one afternoon, a spring of clear emerald water and a gigantic full moon.

It was one of our early safaris and we were still learning from Monty the art of pitching complicated tents with verandas and flies, still hoping nervously (wary of Monty who is meticulous with his equipment) that we hadn't muddled the tent poles again or tangled the guy ropes. We had all the equipment we needed but it had taken time to organize it in such a way that we could make camp with the minimum of frustration and the maximum of efficiency.

Monty, who designed the body of the safari car, fitting it with padded compartments for cameras, and cupboards and compartments and gadgets in every unused space, had also designed a commodious veranda that hooks on to the front of our tent. This we use as kitchen, dining-room and sitting-room. When I arrange the gas cooker and the fridge, the chairs and tables and the safari crates of provisions, I am transported back to my childhood and experience again the old delight of playing houses – the old absorbing satisfaction of making a home and a refuge out of a couple of deck-chairs and a blanket; the instinct must be as old as man.

CIRCLE III

Waking and sleeping in a tent, one is closer to the earth and stars, the thin canvas does not shut them out as totally as the thick walls of a house. And in the morning, one steps straight outside in the dawn. Dawn in the bush is the best time of all, the colours of the sky, the quivering stillness and peace which are a distillation of the hours that follow.

At Samburu, our tents were pitched beneath delicate thorn trees, the small leaves on their fragile branches forming a ceiling of fine green lace. Scattered bushes and dry, wind-blown grass separated us from a gigantic mass of rock sculpted against the sky. There was always a herd of impala nearby, and a lone zebra who seemed to have attached himself to it. There were a couple of waterbuck too, and a vervet monkey that visited us daily, sitting in the branches above our heads. A hundred other animals must have watched us from the concealment of the bushes and on our daily game runs, we saw hundreds more.

From our vantage point on the roof of the safari car (Monty has built a hand-rail round it for protection), rushing through the wind and the sun, the girls and I might see elephant in the distance, a few giraffe or the long ears of a bat-eared fox. Golden brown gerenuk with long, giraffe-like necks flee through the bush, slight and lithe and incredibly graceful. We pass the spring where we get our water, it is clear emerald, the stones at the bottom topaz and saffron and green. A weaver's nest hangs low over our heads, ground hornbills flutter clumsily, their call more like the bleat of a goat than the whistle of a bird. The wide glide of a hawk, the sudden sally of a buffalo weaver – a flick of red, a flash of white like a busy little footballer – the steady beat of the powder-blue wings of the lilac-breasted roller. Burnt umber rocks, honey-coloured grass with the wind tunnelling through it, craggy hills and a wide flung sky and the Ouasa Nyiro river flowing wide and slow. There are elephants upstream and four babies, one of which looks no more than a week old. He fits safe and snug between his mother's stomach and the ground, a miraculous, miniature perfection of herself. We don't see very much of him, the herd keep him securely surrounded, a bunch of admiring, fussing relatives. The big male walks ponderously past; he ignores us, disdains us perhaps. A few of the elephants wallow in the mud, rubbing their flanks leisurely against the cool, soft river bank. A procession of buffalo cross the water, black figures in the silver shallows; Monty photographs them straight into the late afternoon sun. We head for home and Lissa spots a great herd of elephants strung out along the hillside, there must be eighty or ninety of them. They are in single file, hurrying, hurrying; where, why? It is almost dusk and their urgency seems to shroud them in mystery; they disappear into the gathering darkness, the hills falter and dissolve like crumbling pastels.

Amanda, when she was small, used to say of things too numerous to count that they were 'overcountable'. And the moon, as it rises, is 'overdescribable'. It rests on the rim of the earth, a gigantic transparent globule lit by an orange glow from embers burning within. Then the stars appear one by one like pins stuck into a velvet cushion. The camp fire burns brightly, we sit round it after dinner listening to the growling of a lion, the hoot of an owl and the ceaseless cicadas. Suddenly Mandy stands up, then flits into the shadows. She stands perfectly still, watching, then beckons us with silent urgency.

Elephants are passing just behind the tents, about a dozen of them. They move through the shadows with uncanny silence then sail into the moonlight, great grey shadows gliding noiselessly on their endless journeyings. Who can say that their destination and place in the cosmic pattern of things is any more important, any less negligible, than man's? They are gone, passed like ghosts through the silver skein of the bush. Did we imagine them, perhaps?

*

At the Mara, also on the rim of the third circle but on the opposite side from Samburu, we were camped in a clearing on the river bank. It was shaded by tall trees and the water that flowed vigorously past us was flecked with foam and sunlight; the rocky bank opposite was overgrown with thick bush while behind us towered the steep Suria escarpment. I remember particularly the early morning walks along the path at the foot of this escarpment when the long grass was still soaked with dew and glistening in the sun; the school of hippo a little way up the river; the great herds of plains game peacefully grazing on the golden Mara plains – and the lion kill we saw upon them.

The hippos we discovered the first morning of our arrival. We were exploring the path at the foot of the escarpment; there were sudden rustlings in the bush either side of us, little chattering noises, an occasional grunt. A dik-dik, smallest of the antelopes (with the exception of the little suni) and barely more than a foot high, was standing in the middle of the path as though hypnotized, then suddenly raced into the cover of the bush followed by his mate. They never go singly, these dik-dik, perhaps because they are so small and defenceless each acts as sentinel for the other. Leaving the path, we waded hip-high through the dew soaked grass until suddenly we found ourselves on a steep bank above the river. It was wider and deeper here, at this particular point almost like a pool. They had caught sight of us first and were watching us suspiciously, a head or just a pair of eyes and a low forehead protruding out of the water and barely distinguishable from it.

On the opposite bank, an impala was watching us too, head raised alertly, a fine tautness in his glossy flanks and slender neck. To me, the impala is the most beautiful of all the antelope with its rich, chestnut colouring, graceful lines and delicate horns that are wide and lyre shaped. He is a superb jumper as well, clearing a ten foot fence effortlessly and leaping twenty to thirty feet in length.

We stood very still, for hippos are shy creatures – unless you get between them and the water; their means of escape thus blocked they can be viciously dangerous. Assured that we constituted no threat, they continued their sport, leaping and cavorting in the water, sometimes disappearing beneath the surface for a couple of minutes at a time; they are able to remain submerged for as many as four. Like children blowing bubbles they seemed to take pleasure in blowing water from their nostrils in magnificent sprays that glinted in the early sunshine. The hippos could not have been in the river long, for they spend the night feeding, eating their way through two hundred pounds of fodder. Despite their proverbially thick skins, these river horses (as their name means in Greek) are subject to sunburn if they stay away from the water too long; nor beneath the water do their hides protect them from attacks by blood-thirsty leeches. It has long been argued whether hippos walk along river and lake beds or swim, but the question has finally been answered: they swim, and very gracefully too, just as obese people often make the best swimmers or the lightest dancers.

One morning, not far from where the hippos enjoyed their

CIRCLE III

aquasports, we came across two Thompson gazelles engaged in battle. Intent on their conflict, they paid not the slightest attention to us. Horns interlocked, they swung round in a circle, disengaged, then closed in on one another again. Several kongoni watched alongside the female gazelles – perhaps the males were fighting for the harem, or perhaps the dispute was territorial (the Thommies stake their claim to an area by rubbing a glandular secretion from their faces against the grasses and the bushes). There was a pounding of hooves and six zebra galloped past – had they caught the scent of a predator perhaps? Away they raced, the kongoni and the gazelles streaming after them through the grass, their fleetness and freedom of the same substance as the breeze and the light, their swift grace the mobile complement to the stillness of the bush.

As usual, we were carrying no gun – this area is in any case a game reserve – the sound of human voices and the smell of human scent is more of a warning than an invitation. Obviously it would be stupid to take advantage of the fact, to wander unarmed through thick bush and risk walking into a buffalo or a sleeping lion. Although once, in a furious temper, I almost did exactly this, striding blindly out of camp and into the bushes straight past a wounded lion. I didn't see it, but Monty discovered it later. My temper fading as quickly as it had flared and unaware of the lion, I was still in no hurry to return to camp, for it is alone in the bush that one senses most keenly its special beat; the wild wind and the sun seeping into the earth, the fine, taut vibrations of an energy turbulent but controlled, the ceaseless, unseen growth, the endless cycle of birth and death and rebirth.

Alone in the bush, I am more afraid of getting lost than of the game. I have absolutely no sense of direction and I can lose myself, in the dark, between the front door and the garden gate of my own house. On one occasion on the River Mara, I lost myself fifty yards from camp. Night follows swiftly on the heels of the dusk in Africa and suddenly the bushes were enveloped in darkness. I lost the trail I had been following – and with it my nerve. Stumbling into ditches, snagged by branches, glimpsing the golden light of eyes that might have belonged to an antelope or a lion, the relief was immense when I saw a light approaching me, and heard Lissa's voice calling.

The Mara rushed, frothed, eddied, churned round rocks with such exuberant energy it was impossible to hear the usual night sounds above its roar. If lions prowled near the camp of an evening their growls were silenced and we didn't know of their presence till we found their spoor on the path between the tents and the escarpment in the morning. Nor could we hear the maniacal laugh of the hyena, although there were plenty of them in the vicinity and we saw a couple once during the day.

The strange call of a hyena may mean that he is mating, and it may also mean that he is being chased by a lion. The king of beasts seems to loathe these animals and it may be because he is haunted by the presentiment that in his old age, these same hyena who fear him now will pull him to the ground and devour him as they sometimes devour his cubs. The spotted hyena (the striped is far more timorous) is not the coward he is reputed to be, he sometimes hunts in packs and will drag down a wildebeest. He has the strongest jaws of all the mammals and his boldness grows with the night; then he will bite a piece from the limb of a sleeping man. When I sleep out in the open, my blood is more chilled by the cackle of a hyena than the roar of a lion. A lion may simply be curious – but a hyena's visit is

CIRCLE III

always motivated by voracity. There is nothing he won't eat; the male will even devour his own cubs while the female is off her guard. With a quick flick of the paw, he is also able to scoop up a fish from a shallow pool. We knew that although we could not hear the hyenas, they would wait near our camp and scavenge everything we failed to protect, from food to leather camera-cases or shoes.

One afternoon, we found ourselves amongst a pride of lions. We had driven off for the day, stopping in the morning at a Masai manyatta a few miles from the camp. A circle of intertwined branches designed to keep the cattle in at night – and the lions out – surrounded the huts. Three warriors came out to greet us and we followed them into the manyatta. The oblong huts of mud and dung were hardly as high as a man and not much longer. Beside them, women and children stood smiling shyly; the boys had taken the cattle to pasture and would not return till dusk.

The women wore goatskin sarongs and their arms and legs were adorned with iron bracelets, their necks with many beaded necklaces of different colours and designs. Some wore earrings, the mark of a married woman: never during her husband's life time may she take them off, just as many European women never remove their wedding rings. As usual, the small children in the manyatta were quiet and content, although there were no toys to distract them. There is so little crying and fractiousness amongst these children, I have often wondered whether it is not a result of the extra security given them by constant contact with their mothers' backs as babies, and by prolonged breast feeding, sometimes until they are well past two years old.

But there is security in tribalism itself, in the strength of the family unit, in the ties between members of the same age group, and in the very structure of the system itself.

We drove on, stopping later to lunch beneath a large tree. Waving oat grass and scattered trees separated us from a low range of bush-covered hills; it was utterly tranquil. Zebra grazed nearby, a few giraffe wandered past, gentle creatures that rarely attack even when wounded although their kick, should they use it, can be lethal. They give such a strong impression of vagueness it is hardly surprising that the absent-minded mothers even allow their young to wander from one herd to another. The giraffe has a special fascination for me; there is an air of ancient Africa about him, a special link with the living past; there is the slow, graceful awkwardness of his rocking gait, and the way he has of gazing down at you like a large-eyed, dreamy visionary whose head, way up in some rarer sphere, refuses to acknowledge the coarser regions trodden by his feet.

Distracted by the giraffe, we had failed to notice two dots close together in the long grass. They were a little distance away, and slightly darker than the corn-warm colouring of the grass; but we were certain they were the tips of the ears of a lion. The fact that giraffe and zebra had just wandered casually past was no reason to suppose that we were mistaken; they might have been upwind of the predator. Besides, plains game often pass very close to lion when they know that their age-old foe is not hunting, or his attention is concentrated elsewhere.

We got into the safari car and drove slowly to where the two ear tips protruded above the grass. It was a lioness, sitting very still and looking intently ahead of her – in the opposite direction from the giraffe and the zebra who were by now out of sight. Soon we noticed a second lioness about twenty yards in front.

CIRCLE III

And finally we saw that we were flanked by three lions watching from a knoll. They were magnificent creatures with heavy manes; one was lying across the knoll, one was sitting and one standing. All three were staring fixedly ahead in the same direction as the lionesses.

Lions usually make their kill towards dusk, and this was only mid-afternoon; yet the concentrated attention of these animals suggested they might have altered their time-table. We drove within a few yards of the three males, but they barely glanced at us: animals in areas where they are protected soon realize that human beings constitute no threat and react differently from game in hunting blocks. One of the lionesses moved forward, then sat down again in the long grass; she seemed definitely to be stalking something although we could not see what. For some time we waited, and for a while she made no further move. Nor did the lions. But it is always the lionesses who make the kill, retiring immediately afterwards so that their lords and masters may appease their hunger first. If there is insufficient food, they may have to kill again.

The cubs are permitted only what remains when their parents are satiated and it is not at all uncommon to see emaciated cubs, which sometimes even starve to death. Perhaps it is nature's way of operating the checks and balances that control the animal population; too many lions and there would be too few plains game, and too many plains game and there would be insufficient grass. Everything is interdependent on everything else and when man comes along and changes just one natural phenomenon, the delicately balanced interaction of the whole can be thrown out of gear – and usually is.

It may also be that the lionesses feed before their cubs because in order to provide for the whole family, the mothers consume a huge amount of energy and in order to build up this energy they must have nourishment. When not on the kill they are lazy creatures – except when they are in season, then they have been seen to mate between two and three hundred times in two days. . . . But after she has conceived, a lioness will not allow a male to mate with her until her cubs are over eighteen months old and she has taught them how to hunt and fend for themselves. This, combined with the fact that out of a possible six she usually only has a litter of two or more rarely three, acts as a further check on the lion population.

If the pride of five that we were watching included any cubs, the babies would have been left concealed in some safe spot with maternal instructions not to move until after the kill. And we were certain now that the lionesses were on a kill. Both had begun to walk with a certain purposefulness, the very leisureliness of their steps emphasizing the controlled muscles of their bodies and their restrained power. The concentrated tautness of their movement, the wary gleam in their amber eyes – and the intent gaze of the males upon them – indicated that this was no Sunday afternoon stroll. They seemed to be conserving their energy for the concentrated exhausting burst of power they would have to muster in order to catch prey invariably capable of much greater speed than they are themselves; surprise was the element on which they would rely.

They sat down again. Again we waited, but it seemed there would be no action for some time. We drove on past the lionesses through the long grass, looking for the prey which was invisible to us but had probably been scented by the pride. We saw nothing.

We continued driving slowly across the plain with the intention of returning to the lions later on. A little further, and we

CIRCLE III

came across an enormous herd of zebra, there must have been six or seven hundred of them, and many wildebeest as well. The stripes of the zebra were vivid against the silver-greys and laurel greens of the shrubs and trees; no wonder the zebra is so quick to perceive his foe, so fleet to race to safety, he has so poor a camouflage to protect him from his enemies. Today he seemed safe enough. The breeze rippled the long grass and the scene was like a painting in tones of green lit by dusty shafts of gold, for already the light was assuming that glimmering softness which increases with the length of the afternoon. The herds grazed, a bird sang, and it was utterly peaceful.

Suddenly the plain went berserk. Zebra and wildebeest were racing in all directions, some turned in a frantic circle, others streamed away in single file. Zebra were barking and screaming, hoofs were pounding the earth. Then we caught sight of the lionesses. They were tearing across the plain, heading straight towards the panicking herds. Now all the strength in those restrained steps was released in a dynamic eruption of energy whose manifestation was as beautiful to the eye as it was exciting to the senses. The lionesses caught up with a part of the herd and raced through its midst. One of them pounced on a wildebeest and brought it to the ground. The rest of the animals galloped on.

It was still on the plain again. The lionesses walked quietly away from the prey. The males, whom we hadn't noticed in all the excitement, took over. Three yards away, sitting on the roof of our vehicle, we watched while the three lions ripped the wildebeest to pieces. They were too absorbed in their meal to pay any attention to us, although every so often one of them glanced up, a glare of warning in his wild eyes.

The lionesses were sitting motionless in the grass some ten

yards off like well trained dogs. They didn't move until the males, satiated now and drowsy, ceased eating and rolled on to their sides, panting from their orgy. Then it was their turn, and their patience was rewarded. After the lions, the hyena would come, and after the hyena, the vultures; nature allows of no waste.

There is so much still to learn and understand about the game, and the facts we do know are merely a key to the pitch of an unknown theme. Joy Adamson is convinced that animals use extra-sensory perception, so that the young cubs left by a lioness on a kill know when to emerge from cover by a telepathic message. Joy is certain that messages of this kind can be communicated as far as a hundred miles. It is easier to explore the moon than the mind of an animal – or the mind of a man.

We drove back to camp. A Masai chief and several elders were waiting there for us. We sat in a semi-circle by the river with them, drinking beer, and the chief told us of the new wheat scheme soon to be implemented near the Mara. So it was finally happening. The nomads were turning farmers (as they must) and one day brick houses and ugly towns would spring up on the wild free plains where once the zebra and giraffe roamed, and the oat-grass grew tall and gold.

One day, there would be no more bush. It would be ripped up with shining black roads and even the most secret corner would be penetrated by naked neon lights. There would be nothing left to discover and no place to escape.

A romantic's view, I am generally told. I am a romantic, unashamed and devout, but applied in this case the term merely reflects the predominant values of the West. Since childhood our attitudes have been set into rigid moulds by our parents, our teachers, our TV sets and our radios, and imprisoned within these moulds we cannot conceive of a life which is motivated by values different from those we have been taught to accept. If the president of a country were to give priority to the search for Truth, to the promotion of the arts and learning, and the preservation of beauty everyone would think he had gone raving mad! Our evaluations are economic – not in the interests of 'progress', but in the interest of power (all is not vanity, it is also power), which is the underlying motive, often unconscious, of many actions of most individuals and nearly all nations. And seeing that it is in the interests of economics, and we will never put any consideration before economics, the bush will one day vanish and 'go under' as old Chief Batian would have said. And if there are those who think that this matters, and that the implications are enormous, and that 'no people' as Camus wrote in his *Carnets*, 'can live outside beauty', what can they do but stand high on a hill and blow against the wind?

CIRCLE IV

The Diminishing Band

SOMETHING else is disappearing with the tribes and the game: it is a small number of white men who belong to the diminishing band of self-sufficient people in the world. Up at Meru, and still further away from home at Kora Hill, we met several such individuals living and working in the bush.

A friend from the States who was in a hurry had chartered a single-engined plane and we flew off to Meru with him. Great African clouds billowed round us like snow drifts, the terraced hills and steep valleys of the Kikuyu below were lush green and studded with pools of water like giant pearls. But a safari is not really a safari if you fly. You see that the earth below is green or that it is brown, that it is hilly or it is flat – you see, but you do not feel. It is like looking at a rose for the first time through a hot-house window and being told: 'this flower has a sweet perfume and its petals feel like velvet', but you never actually smell or touch it. And when you reach your destination, it is like standing in the room of a house without having walked through the gardens or even along the corridors and up the stairs that lead to it. But flying round a country instead of driving is symptomatic of the labour-saving, time economizing, antiseptic, conveyor-belt world we live in; it is the difference between sugar that has been refined in the factory (no dirt, no sweat, no dust), and the succulent juice of the sugar cane that has been freshly cut in the fields.

CIRCLE IV

As a child, I had come to know every nook and cranny of the woods and hills that surrounded my home, penetrating them on horseback. In a car, you can see the main features of a country but you cannot feel its atmosphere. Driving and flying are all part of our diminishing contact with nature, and that growing depersonalization which is the result of the use of machines, and of mass manufactured goods.

In the end, flying to Meru lost us time instead of gaining it. The little air-strip was half under water, and a landing too risky; the pilot nosed upwards again and we turned back towards Nairobi. It was a big disappointment for neither the girls nor I had ever been to Meru; besides, we had planned to camp next to George Adamson and his lions, a long standing invitation which we had somehow not got around to accepting. When Monty suggested we transfer our luggage from the plane to the safari car, drive as far as the foothills of Mount Kenya, spend the night at the Mount Kenya Safari Club and continue on to Meru early the next morning, the rest of us enthusiastically seconded the plan.

Once upon a time, the Club was a private house. Then it was turned into a beautiful but unpretentious hotel which in those days was called Mawingo, Swahili for clouds. It seemed to me the perfect name, for it is seven and a half thousand feet high and faces straight on to the snowy peaks of Kerinyaga. The air, in the early morning, is Alpine in its silence and its purity, and one feels closer than usual to the sky. There is a swimming-pool between you and the mountain now, and artificial lakes. But it is still very beautiful and when we arrived just before dusk, we could still see the forest-clad foothills beyond the smooth, generous slopes of lawn. The mountain, as it so often is, was wrapped in cloud.

It is ritual, when we are at the Club, to step out of bed and cross to the window to see if the mountain has made its daybreak appearance, like some aloof monarch that steps momentarily on to the balcony for the crowds. The following morning, just after six, Kerinyaga revealed itself, its remote pinnacles high and ethereal in a dreaming sky.

Outside, the early morning air was crisp and clear (at night, it is so cold a fire burns in every bedroom) and the girls had run down to the bird sanctuary by the artificial lakes. Marabou storks watched like gluttonous old gentlemen with pot-bellies and no necks; Egyptian geese waddled past, white ibis flew overhead and an owl stared from the branches of a tree, still as a wood carving on a totem pole. Near the rose gardens are monkeys and parakeets, while peacocks cry and strut across the lawns. Several hundred acres belonging to the Club have been made into a game ranch and here eland and impala, giraffe and buffalo roam; the wooded foothills of Kerinyaga that begin where the smooth lawns end, are full of buffalo.

Lissa and I cast wistful glances towards the stables; we were longing to ride, in that invigorating air, down by the fast flowing stream that rushes through tunnels of bamboo, or out in the open within sight of the vast brown plains and tawny hills of the north. But we had to leave immediately after breakfast; there was no telling how long it would take us to get to Meru across that rain sodden countryside.

It was dry at first. Dust billowed behind us and soon we began to descend towards the sun-filled distances of the north – for Monty and me the most exciting part of all Kenya. Then we checked our descent and took a sharp turn along the road to Meru. Soon we found ourselves sliding through thick, glutinous mud. Now, on either side of us, there was luxuriant forest, cool and green as a few miles back the hills had been sun-seeped and charred. We pushed our way through this mud, skidding and slithering the entire way to Meru. The last ten miles were like a narrow chute between tall hedges with just sufficient room between them for a single vehicle to pass. We had no fear of meeting anyone else; there was only one possible direction in which to travel – down.

We finally arrived at Leopard Rock and the home of the game warden, Peter Jenkins. Peter told us that the road to George's was impassable (we were not exactly surprised) and the lorry with all our equipment, which had fortunately arrived the day before, prior to the last heavy fall of rain, had stopped on the river bank near Leopard Rock.

Six white rhino awaited us in camp. White rhino are much milder by nature than black, but these were completely tame. They had been sent up from South Africa and because these creatures are now rare, they were constantly guarded by a game ranger; hence their friendliness to human beings. They were not of course 'white', they simply had squarish lips instead of pointed (they are called in Afrikaans *wyd* lipped which means 'wide' lipped – not white) so that they browse as well as graze. And there is too this difference in temperament.

Far more aggressive than the rhino are the crocodile which haunt the banks of the river that runs through Meru Game Park. It was narrow where we were camped, very narrow; I would never have thought a crocodile would even have bothered to slither into the water between its banks. Nor did we see one, either in the river or out, but we learnt afterwards that the crocodiles in this area don't even lie waiting for man: they actually hunt him.

The crocodiles left us alone and the rhinos were unobtrusive –

but the elements went berserk. That night, there broke one of the most violent storms I have ever experienced. I lay in bed watching a framework of branches against a sky that was disturbingly light instead of the usual purple or black, and listened to the wind pattering gently against the sides of the tent. Then clap upon clap of thunder began exploding above our heads. The world flared with cosmic bursts of brilliance and the wind careened dementedly round the tents, flaying the rain against the canvas. We were camped amongst tall trees; I waited for one to fall across the tents with each fresh clap of thunder and each vivid white flood of light that followed it.

There was a climax to that storm. It came in one ear-splitting explosion when it seemed that all the world had been rolled into a cannon ball and fired into my head. I shut my eyes and stopped breathing, certain that the tree had fallen at last and killed us all.

I opened my eyes and the trees were all standing; more important still, so were the tents. I could see them in that strange grey light, and I could see them too in the bursts of lightning. We thought that the girls must be petrified and Monty waded through the water to see how they were surviving this night of violence; but they seemed more elated than scared.

The rain fell all night and I began to feel as though an impregnable wall of water were shutting me off from the rest of the world. It was a feeling I was familiar with and I didn't particularly like it. I had experienced it a few years before during the floods. By night I had listened to an incessant drumming of water on sodden earth; by day I had looked out at teeming rain wrapped tightly round the house like a cocoon of silk. There was the same insistent drumming now and the pools outside the tent were beginning to merge into a grey pond which slowly spread itself across the earth like some vast, phantasmagoric octopus. Reluctantly I stretched out an arm and touched the floor of the tent; it was dry. I would not have to evacuate all our possessions to the safari car. There was not a leak in the canvas either, we could not say the same of our roof at home when the rains came. . . .

Morning brought a clouded sky inlaid with gleams of sunlight. The girls and I walked barefoot through the deep mud, it was soft and cool, the going far easier and pleasanter than with shoes. The sun penetrated the cloud, the earth steamed, and by midday the mud was already beginning to dry out. We decided to try and drive over to George Adamson's that afternoon; Peter Jenkins, the game warden wanted to see George too, and we went in convoy.

The path had turned into a muddy canal. We slid and skidded and stuck, then skidded and slid and stuck again. Where the water lay deepest, we made a semi-circular detour, crashing through the bush – I don't think any of us expected to reach George's, but we were enjoying the attempt. We managed to make the seven miles to the ford, but then we found that this normally shallow stream had been transformed into a wide and foaming river. The other side a bulldozer waited helplessly, a few of Peter's workers standing beside it. Ironically enough, they had been engaged in making a new path through the bush.

Taking a stick to test the depth of the water, Peter waded carefully to the other side. They are dangerous, these flooded fords and rivers, almost every year a person or a car is swept away by the force of their currents. The bulldozer was heavy and had a high clearance, and Peter managed to guide it across the water.

We of course were forced to turn back. We stuck yet again – this time outside Joy Adamson's abode. This was the period in her life when she was living alone in the bush attempting to return her cheetah Pippa to the wild. But we mustn't mention Pippa, Peter warned us, she had been missing with her cubs for some days and Joy was deeply disturbed.

She did not show it though and we received a warm, enthusiastic welcome from her. She was delighted to have guests – no, no, it didn't matter how many we were, we must come in and have a drink. We were lucky to find her organized again, for three weeks when the river flooded its banks, she had been living in her Land-Rover! What would we have – tea, coffee, beer? If only she had a greater selection to offer us – wait, she would fetch something to sit on, and a table. Netta would help her carry everything under the tamarind tree on the river bank – where was she, why didn't she come – had we met her? She hailed from America and was staying with her, acting secretary for a while. Monty knew Netta, certainly, she had come all the way from America to get to Joy and then her money had nearly run out and she had appeared in his office (as people are always appearing in his office) for help and advice.

With tremendous nervous energy, Joy rushed to and fro carting boxes, chairs, tables and a crate of beer to the river bank, refusing help, scattering plates of peanuts around, and talking quickly the while with vivacious and enthusiastic volubility. Netta appeared, all calm and serene. We sat down beneath the beautiful tamarind tree whose foliage formed a cool green Gothic ceiling above our heads while its branches trailed in the

CIRCLE IV

fast flowing stream contained once more between the steep, grassy banks. A few yards back from the river stood two little shacks of wood and thatch, there was a table and a few chairs in one, and a couple of beds in the other. I knew that it was through choice and not through hardship that Joy lives so simply – at this time, I knew little else about her. Later on, we were to become friends.

The second time I met Joy she was living at Lake Naivasha. The simply furnished but spacious living-room opened out completely on to the veranda (Joy hates to be confined and 'Born Free' is a very apt title for a woman whose prime need is to be next to nature) with a view of graceful thorn trees and the water. One or two of her portraits of African tribesmen were hanging on the walls, and a few of her exquisite paintings of flowers. But she was unable at the time to command the customary fineness of touch with her brush, she could not play the piano, and she could only type with one finger of her left hand: she had seriously injured the right one in a motor car accident. Not many months before this, her beloved cheetah, Pippa, had broken her leg and as a result of the injury, died. Yet despite all this, I found myself talking to a woman who had just discovered a new attitude towards life during the past few years of semi-exile in the bush whilst rehabilitating her 'Spotted Sphinx'.

It seemed to me that during this time at Meru Joy had found herself on the threshold of some new understanding, about to make the first step, as it were, into a sphere of intelligence that is on quite a different plane from our own. And in making this approach she began to feel with growing conviction that the only hope of man's survival in a world which he is slowly destroying is to learn from the animals – who will *not* destroy themselves; and who will continue to live because they know *how* to continue – providing man does not eliminate them. These are not Joy's words, it is simply the gist of a thought to which she returned several times.

She had asked me to lunch three minutes after I set foot in the house with the same hospitality she showed us at Meru. I had refused, partly not wishing to impose, partly because I had expected to have to make small-talk. We were virtually strangers, having barely exchanged two words during that first meeting at her camp. Two minutes more, and we were deep in conversation. I stayed to lunch, and I stayed to tea as well, I drank innumerable cups of coffee and left – almost six hours later.

During that time, Joy made many remarks of consequence and I kept thinking that in her next book she should write not simply about animals but about herself.

Joy has millions of admirers and a few close friends. She is an extremist whose refusal to compromise is fiercely absolute. She is an idealist whose ebullient convictions do not tolerate standards lower than her own. She is an individual of inexhaustible energy and enormous determination which drive her hard – and often tempestuously – towards her goal.

Sometimes, in a crowd scene in a painting, there are figures that are strongly delineated and colourfully painted so that they stand out from the others. In life, the definite lines and undiluted colours which make such individualists arresting are a mixture of large qualities – and therefore correspondingly large faults. You are attracted to them for their qualities, or turned away by their faults, and there is no in-between.

That afternoon with Joy at Naivasha, the salient characteristics of this talented woman which attracted me the most were her sincerity, her penetrating intelligence and a great curiosity about life generated by an unflagging energy for the struggle to live fully – and in consequence, to grow.

The afternoon at Meru when first I met Joy, conversation centred round Meru Park, which Joy was aiding unstintingly from the Elsa Fund, and the possibility of filming *Living Free* (which later materialized). Before we left, Joy gave Peter some seeds from the tamarind tree; boiled in water, she said, they were wonderfully soothing for scorpion bites – and Peter's wife had been bitten by one the previous evening. We promised to pass by and pick her up on our way to George's the following day.

We stopped at the Jenkins' house before returning to camp. The cottage stands above a steep, stone-strewn bank at the foot of which the river rushes cool and clear. The roof leaks, the floors are all uneven and the sitting-room runs into the veranda, the veranda into the garden so that there is a delightful vagueness where one begins and the other ends. Geraniums hanging from the ceiling add to this confusion and you find yourself wondering whether the sitting-room has drawn the garden inside itself or the garden has drawn the sitting-room in.

Wicked little monkeys leap unbidden on to the table and dash off with a banana or an apple – exasperating Peter's wife Sara; the nearest market was many miles away and the road either rutted or muddy. She jumped up and shooed them outside, then went to look for little Mark. But Mark had gone with his father – he was always going with his father. She sighed, she wanted to teach him to read but he preferred the animals in the park to the letters in the book – had we seen the old buffalo that browsed round the house? He stayed within a few yards of it and never harmed anyone; perhaps he was aware that no one was going to harm him and had come to realize, now that he was old, there was in fact protection in this strange, voluntary association with human beings.

Peter, tall, blue-eyed, energetic, capable, returned with Mark in tow, took off the battered ancient hat he favoured and told us that the Park officials were granting him a new house. Sara, very English, slight, with blue eyes and fine fair hair, was delighted; all last night during the storm the roof had leaked on to her bed; the baby had been sick and when she got out of bed to attend to it she had trodden upon the scorpion – the pain, as it always is, had been excruciating. Peter talked of the new road he planned to make through the Park and of the game lodge he would like to see there. He talked intently and it was obvious that his work was of vital interest to him.

Back at camp, only a few yards from the tents, a cheetah was sitting in the grass. She did not move as we approached closer and we knew then it must be one of Joy's. Any other cheetah would have raced away from us with that breathtaking suppleness and speed so beautiful to watch – fleetest of the game, a cheetah can run as fast as sixty miles an hour.

The next morning, when we picked Joy up *en route* for George's, we learnt that the cheetah had returned to Joy's camp and was one of Pippa's offspring.

This time, we managed to cross the ford. A flooded river will often subside in the course of a few hours, once the rain has ceased, and it had not rained the entire night. Now the sun was hot and the breeze blew billowing clouds across the sky; one more day and instead of sliding through the mud we would be jolting over back-breaking ruts and bumps.

George welcomed us with his usual shy reserve. Quiet,

CIRCLE IV

philosophical, simple in his tastes and the way in which he chooses to live, he sat with us on the veranda of his little wood and thatch abode. Overhead, nests hung from the branches of the thorn trees beneath which George had built his home, and countless golden weavers fluttered amongst the leaves. He maintains they come to human habitation because they find protection there from their enemies, the snakes.

That first meeting, it was George's serenity that struck me the most forcibly, the serenity of a man who has learnt to live alone and who has gleaned with the years a philosophy which satisfies him. Not that I have ever discussed such matters with George; one can talk to him about his lions or about the early days in Kenya or his safaris to Lake Rudolf, but when it comes to more personal matters one respects his reserve. His white hair and beard and the frequently distant expression in his strikingly blue eyes enhances his philosopher's demeanour. But he is essentially a man of action.

Every now and then, a little absentmindedly, he would take a handful of seeds and toss them on the ground; immediately a flock of little yellow birds would flutter down. 'When will the lions come, George,' the girls kept asking, 'when will the lions come?' And George would smile his patient smile (he must have been asked the question a thousand times before), look towards a rocky hillock as though he were unconsciously waiting for someone to come home and answer in his slow, patient way; 'I never can tell. They come and go, you know.'

He was still rehabilitating his lions at this time and the experiment seemed to be nearing a successful conclusion. But there were to be one or two unexpected developments before its completion.

While he was at Meru, he had had the satisfaction of seeing

his lions completely adapt themselves to the life of a wild pride. At the same time, they didn't forget their old friend but retained their trust in him and came to visit him frequently – an incredible and unique situation. A wonderfully fulfilling end to the story for George, too. But . . . unlike George, visitors to the Park were unable to tell the difference between his lions and the others. Even if they could, not everyone welcomes the company of a powerful, fully-grown lion. This was the first problem.

The second was the result of a well-known leonine trait, these animals are fascinated by – or dislike – children. Their eyes follow them incessantly, flicking back and forth as the child darts to and fro. One day, Peter was driving in his open vehicle in the Park with Sara and their son Mark. They met George, with Boy. Peter stopped to greet George. Boy strolled over, lunged through the open side of the car across Sara and bit Mark's arm. Peter managed to switch on the engine – his arm beneath Boy's body – and shoot off, leaving the lion behind.

Mark's arm healed, but there arose a storm of controversy. Whose fault was it? George's? Peter's? The lion's? Some said George should have terminated his relationship with his lions by throwing thunder flashes at them, so that they would have kept away from him – and all human beings. Others said that Peter should not have driven round the Park with Mark in an open car (to follow this to its logical conclusion, he would then have had to change his car and stockade his house and garden). I also heard someone express the opinion that such an accident should not in any way be allowed to stop the progress of a unique experiment of world-wide interest; it was incidental to it but I cannot imagine anyone adopting this outlook if the threatened child happened to be his own.

The result of the affair was that George had to remove Boy from Meru Game Park and find some place else to release him. But meantime, Boy broke his leg. Vets flew up to Meru and operated on him, then George flew Boy to Naivasha, where Joy was already established. The wound began to heal but still George had found no place to rehabilitate Boy that was mutually agreeable to him and the Kenya Government. Monty was very involved in trying to obtain this permission for George, but the difficulty lay in finding an area where there were neither people nor cattle, tourists nor hunters. Just as George was beginning to despair, he received permission to take Boy to Kora Hill.

Kora Hill or Where the Road Runs Out, I thought when we went there. It overflows beyond the rim of the fourth circle – but then it seems to lie beyond the rim of anywhere. It is the most desolate terrain I have ever crossed in this country, more desolate than the desert and semi-desert of the north, because colourless and unexciting. Mile upon mile we drove across flat, grey countryside covered in thick thorn bushes that looked charred and lifeless. The last seventy miles took us five hours; the narrow path winding through the bushes was so uneven and rutted, it felt at times as though the vehicle was about to keel over on its side. Even George has been lost in this terrain, and this is some measure of its monotony. George had left one or two exotic indications of the route: mostly toilet paper wrapped round a branch, 'You can't miss it' he'd said, 'there's a dried up water pan after the path forks right. That's Redojari. A few miles further on, there's another one. That's –' (some place that sounded like Timbuctoo but was a lot less likely). Fortunately

Monty's sense of direction, combined with the toilet paper and the dried up water pans and George's vague directions finally got us to our destination.

Just before we arrived, the countryside began to undulate slightly, the sand was scattered with russet coloured pebbles and white quartz, the bush thinned out a little. The path even wound through a wild green forest. Then we saw the doum palms, African heralds of water. Tents were pitched amongst them on the river bank – not George's; his was three miles back in amongst the thorn bushes and craggy hillocks of rock.

To explain the presence of the tents, it is necessary to mention yet another development that had taken place between my first meeting with George at Meru, and this safari to Kora Hill.

Two swinging young Australians living in London had bought a lion cub from Harrods and were rearing it in the curiosity shop in which they worked. Lions who live in curiosity shops are faced with two alternatives when they grow up: either they go to zoos – or they are repatriated to the bush by a George Adamson. Christian, the fifth generation London lion, was extremely fortunate. Bill Travers of *Born Free* happened to walk into the shop one day and make the young lion's acquaintance, whereupon he suggested George might rehabilitate the London lion with Boy at Kora Hill. The whole unlikely story materialized and Bill filmed it.

One of the tents amongst the fringe of doum palms was his; another belonged to the owners of the London lion, John Rendall and Ace Burke (with whom Lissa and Mandy, and Monty and I were all to become good friends and with whom we were to share many a laugh both on that safari and later on in Nairobi); another belonged to George's brother Terence Adamson, and the couple that remained to the rest of the

CIRCLE IV

minimal film unit. Monty was associate producer, and now his tent stood with the others on the banks of the River Tana. As for George, he was banished three miles back in amongst the thorn bushes and the massive outcrops of slabs of rocks and stones. His brother Terence had been busy building a compound for Boy, and another alongside it for Christian. Soon he and George would build a couple of wooden huts and here they would live with only the lions for company after the departure of the little film unit in a few weeks' time. Eventually, George would be completely on his own for it would take him a couple of years to rehabilitate Christian. Accustomed to London pavements, the young lion could not even walk three yards without flopping down and waiting with helpless pathos for someone to take the thorns out of his tender paws. The most affectionate, sweet-natured animal I have ever come across, after playing with him at Kora Hill it is difficult to imagine Christian fighting ferocious wild lions for his territorial rights, or for his mate.

Not only would George be alone with his lions, but during the rainy seasons he would be completely cut off from the rest of the world. The roads then would be impassable. I had spent half a day at a supermarket in Nairobi getting together enormous packages of food to keep him stocked up for a while. We would see he did not starve – but what if he fell ill? He didn't even have a two-way transmitter radio at this time. Patient, imperturbable, George doesn't worry about things like that. He has lived on his own too often, and in places equally as remote as Kora Hill.

Kenya is a spawning ground for unlikely situations and unlikely people: there is scope for individualism and there is frequently a challenge. Many of the early settlers came here because they were dissatisfied with life in their country of origin or because they had rebelled against banality or routine or convention. Or simply because they were in search of adventure.

I cannot imagine George Adamson living a conventional, routine life. They say that if you put a Masai in jail, he slowly withers and dies. I think if you confined George in a city and chained him to a desk, he would wither and die just like a Masai. I think his brother Terence would too.

He has the same white hair as George, the same strikingly blue eyes, the same white bushy eyebrows. But his face is craggier, not so clean cut as George's and he talks in rather erratic bursts, instead of his brother's slower, more hesitant way of expressing himself. Each has a doggedness and a philosophy which I believe has been crystallized out of the earth and the sky, the wind and the stars to which they have been so close all their lives.

Terence is a natural botanist. There wasn't a flower, a tree or a shrub whose name he didn't know at Kora Hill; henna is extracted from one of the plants he showed us, incense from another. I sat talking with him of an evening amongst the doum palms, the wide river flowing steadily past, the sky alight with stars. Less retiring than George, he says what he thinks with a blunt honesty, desiring neither your support nor caring if you condemn him either. It is as though his self-sufficiency and independence are carried over into the way in which he expresses himself. He is completely without artifice; priest or prince, beggar or millionaire, it doesn't make the slightest bit of difference to him. Monty once remarked that he is a humble man. Humble is not a word that particularly appeals to me, perhaps I associate it with Uriah Heep; but in a man of the

CIRCLE IV

earth like Terence, the word is probably applicable to the modesty of his demands and his expectations.

Once, after dinner, he was standing by the table and unthinkingly put his hand in a pocket of which so little remained that all five fingers and his knuckles too came straight out the other side. He wasn't even aware of it. I couldn't join in the laughter, there was something Chaplinesque in the situation – and yet not Chaplinesque at all because for Terence there was no pathos in the situation whatsoever. He simply said vaguely – without even bothering to remove his hand and not the suggestion of a smile on his face: 'Oh. It's the thorns, you know.' I don't believe he had any idea why the others were laughing – certainly he wasn't the least bit concerned: clothes, these people's values, what did they matter?

Elephants matter to Terence. They matter as much to him, almost, as lions do to George. He told me that when he was working up at Marsabit, if an elephant blocked his path, he would simply get out of his vehicle, approach it, ask it to move on – maybe even pat it – and the elephant would obligingly lumber off. The story may sound far-fetched but I have heard his strange relationship with these animals substantiated from two different sources.

Terence was re-cutting an earth road through the bushes as far as Kora Hill so that George and the little film unit could get there. (That is why I came to think of it as Kora Hill or Where the Road Runs Out.) It was hot, and he was tired at the end of the day, one saw that he was growing old. But he has retained the glee of a schoolboy with the distant philosophic gaze of his brother. And like George too he is gleaning, as he grows older, the fruits of an African harvest.

Joy, George, Terence, Peter and Sara all belong to the

diminishing band of self-sufficient people in the world. People who are able to make their own amusements, treat their own ailments, teach their own children, bake their own bread and enjoy their own company, to manage in fact with few of the props and aids of the twentieth century.

I admire people who are able to lead such lives, but the bush and the city are two extremes and I find that I need them both. The treble grows dull without the bass – how exciting the skyscrapers after my thorn trees, how stimulating the vital, noisy breathless, brash turbulent whirl of New York! Here, in the harshest of all cities, is the greatest antithesis to the bush and perhaps it is for this reason it holds an attraction for me – even though I could not stay there for very long. And if it does not possess the beauty of Florence or the antiquity of Jerusalem or the mellow graciousness of certain parts of London, it is still, like those other cities, a great storehouse of all the best things that man has achieved, the art and the music and the literature, the discoveries and the learning, the rich residue bequeathed by him over the centuries. In the bush, man communicates with nature, but it is only in the city that man can communicate with man.

The city itself is a gigantic complex of communications from the planes and the buses, the trains and the cars to the radios and the newspapers, the cinemas and the theatre and the television, from the paintings that hang in the galleries and the books that line the shelves, or the music that fills the concert halls to the packed cubicles of habitation where people live in such close proximity they are within calling distance of one another.

But the closer they live together the less they call and the fainter grows their cry. It is as though the cords of the incredibly complex network are tightening and cutting people off both from the diminishing outside resources – and from one another as well.

It is the inevitable paradox whereby the greatest creativity is by its very nature capable of the greatest destructivity so that the substances developed by the scientists in the cities' seats of research to cure and to heal are at the same time diverted to genocidal purposes; or the closer people live together and the greater their opportunity to communicate, the more widely they become separate and even alienated. In the cities, mutual assistance, hospitality and that central, basic foundation from which springs all else – the family unit, are slowly disintegrating; in the desert and the bush they are paramount.

Where the bush is primitive the city is sophisticated, and where the city is barbaric the bush has its civilization, and only in a synthesis of what each has to offer is there a possibility of progress and harmonious living.

CIRCLE V

The Elephant and Us

FROM the rim of the second circle all the way to the sea and the desert on the outermost circumference of the seventh, paths are woven by the secret coming and goings of the elephant. Approaching him on foot is like coming face to face with a symbol of the power and antiquity of Africa herself. It is a symbolic confrontation of the beginning and the end of things too, for although these creatures have a timelessness about them, rooted as they are in centuries long past, today their time is running out. Perhaps that is why I sense a sadness in the creature's majesty and a pathos in those small, wise, long-lashed eyes set deep in skin as wrinkled as parched earth; perhaps too it is because I know that eventually my species will destroy theirs. There is a terrible betrayal here for the responsibility is entirely ours, and yet the betrayal is inevitable as long as we continue to multiply our numbers and overflow into territory which once belonged to the animals. In this head-on confrontation which has suddenly arisen in the last couple of decades, it is not only the fate of the elephant which is at stake; it is, I believe, of significance in the destiny of mankind. For if we push the king of beasts under and he becomes extinct, man will have destroyed one more link in the umbilical cord between himself and nature without which, any more than a foetus in its mother's womb, he cannot survive.

Partly because of the strangeness of its habits, partly because

CIRCLE V

of what appears to be a more highly developed intelligence, and partly because he is imbued with a certain mystery, the elephant has a special fascination for Monty and me. And this past year we have been very much involved with this, the largest and yet the most patient of all the beasts, sometimes following him along ancient routes that he has trodden through the bush as far back and further than the Bronze Age.

This involvement, eighteen years after his arrival back home in Kenya, had completed a personal circle of Monty's own, for it has brought him back to his first love, elephant and zoology.

To explain how he finally arrived there, it is necessary to follow the chain of cause and effect all the way back to a couple of mules and the foundation of his father's business over fifty years ago; and it is perhaps interesting to go back still further in order to explain how his father happened to come to East Africa at all.

Monty's grandfather was born in the Russian Ukraine. A man of large frame, long beard, dominating temperament and a citizen of some standing in the community, he had been given the privilege bestowed on a small percentage of Jews of full citizenship. This favour had been granted him, together with a piece of land, after twenty-five years of service in the Russian army. As a civilian, he earned his living by buying bales of cloth and parcelling them out to tailors and dressmakers; the clothes they brought back to him he subsequently sold.

He built four houses on his land, and Monty's father spent his childhood in one of them. There were cows and chickens – and of course a cherry orchard (although my father-in-law is more *au fait* with Gogol than Chekov; Gogol was born in the neighbouring town).

Only ten per cent of the Jews living in Russia at this time

were allowed to go to school. However, a Russian general living in my father-in-law's town considered the Jews had had a raw deal after their contribution to the Russian war and obtained permission to open a school unbound by discriminatory laws. It was this school that Eddie Ruben attended.

But anti-Semitism there certainly was and continued to be. Partly for this reason, partly to escape the three years' compulsory military service, a member of the family living in one of the four houses built by the old patriarch, decided to leave Russia. He went to East Africa – perhaps because in those days there was always the hope that in Africa one would find gold. He bought a farm, and he wrote to Monty's grandparents to join him. Monty's grandfather remained behind to settle his affairs, and his mother went ahead with her four sons, going to Palestine *en route*. There she stayed with two of her sons 'to give them a little Jewish education'. Monty's father, then aged fourteen, and his sixteen year old brother continued their journey to Kenya. For a couple of years they lived with their uncle on what must have been one of the first European farms in this country. Then World War I broke out. Their father was caught in Russia and now could not leave, and their mother and two brothers were prisoners of the Turks in Palestine. Fortunately the Turks didn't want female or child prisoners and so sent them to Egypt, then under British rule. From Egypt they finally made their way to Kenya. At this point Monty's mother, a still good looking woman well-known for her prowess as a horticulturist (her father also left Russia for reasons of anti-Semitism and came here via Palestine), finally interrupts the story with nostalgic eagerness. Six or seven years old at the time, she remembers the arrival of Monty's grandmother vividly. She went with her parents to the station in a rickshaw to meet and make welcome 'another Jewish family', but what impressed her most of all about the strangers were the red Egyptian fezes worn by the two small Ruben brothers as they stepped out of the train.

Their two older brothers had joined the British army – Monty's father lying about his age in order to do so. He worked with oxen and mules (from the stories he tells it would seem he enjoyed it) and when the war ended he bought a couple of the mules and a couple of carts as well, and founded Express Transport. He became so totally involved in its development, today Express Transport is Eddie Ruben and Eddie Ruben is Express Transport. Pioneer, patriot, steadfast member of Kenya's tiny Jewish community and staunch supporter of Rotary, Freemasonry and the British Legion, he delights in his goldfish and a game of poker. He has somehow never lost his Russian accent and it is very much a part of the local 'character' for which he is known; nor would the jokes he likes to tell or his fund of anecdotes sound the same without it. Amongst his stories are many fables which he has a habit of using to illustrate his reasoning in preference to logic. With his strong hands, his blue eyes and his ruddy complexion, he makes one feel he should really have been a farmer in the Ukraine – although both his younger brothers farmed in Kenya.

He owned a farm himself once. It was slung nine thousand feet high in the hills and it was for me a case of love at first sight. I have always wanted to own land, ever since I was a child, and this was some of the most beautiful I had ever seen – or have ever seen since. There was a pretty chestnut gelding as well; he had slender legs and a proud, high head and I used to ride him every morning before breakfast when the air up there was frost-sharp and the silence like splintered glass. He was called Masara and we used to go, Masara and I, way over that tumbling mass of hills which always seemed to me so near the sky. But the farm, to my great sadness, was sold and with it the cattle and the pigs and the horses amongst which Monty's father, in his old felt hat, always seemed so much at home.

By now a fleet of lorries and a petrol tanker had replaced the faithful mules and the office had overflowed into a travel bureau, a coffee warehouse, and later on with the advent of tourists, a touring company. As for the film companies, this side of the business goes back to *Trader Horn* which was made here in the 1920s. The principal actress was Edwina Booth. My father-in-law says that he remembers the name because the movie-makers caused such a stir in the tiny, remote township of Nairobi. My own opinion is that he remembered her because she was a very pretty woman!

Today the film companies still need advice and help in finding suitable locations and familiarizing themselves with conditions at first very strange to them. It was really through personal contact that Monty began to build up this department of the business without, in the early stages, being actually aware of it. The Hollywood film industry is a small circle and reputation spreads by word of mouth. Soon, he found himself frequently being drawn into the production in more than an advisory capacity; so that one day when Simon Trevor walked into his office and stated without preamble that he wanted to make a film about elephants, he committed himself immediately. He now had both the necessary contacts and a certain amount of experience behind him. His imagination was fired and he was full of enthusiasm. At last he was tackling a project that stimulated his real interests, satisfied a creative need and utilized his ability. If he had not been able to study elephant as he liked, here at least was an opportunity to present a unique record of these animals. There was too a certain urgency in the project; that urgency which lies in the transience of so much in this country.

When finally Monty had raised the interest and the finance a long cherished ambition of Simon's was also realized; he would now be able to work on his own. And not for just a week or a month, but for an entire year.

When Simon Trevor talks about his work, his blue eyes become intent and he is carried away with enthusiasm. One senses the single-mindedness and dogged determination – which doubtless at times amounts to sheer stubbornness – then suddenly he relaxes with a humorous remark and an infectious grin. He has that toughness and self-sufficiency which frequently typifies men in this country because their jobs demand it and their lives give them the scope to utilize it. He is also a talented photographer and possesses the many ingredients necessary to film game well in this country. He has, first and foremost, a wide knowledge and experience of the animals gained during the year he was a game warden. He knows what to wait for, where and when. Dogged, compact and self-reliant, he goes off into the bush for months on end with his tent, his photography equipment – and his Danish wife, Laila.

Her fair hair bleached from the sun, her athletic body deeply tanned, she is his assistant cameraman, his game spotter, his clapper boy, his typist and his cook. Calm and efficient, sensible and organized, she is also a trained nurse, a profession she qualified for in Denmark just before she came here. She and Simon live in the bush more than they live in their house, but when the elephant film was being made they were under canvas almost continuously for over a year.

It materialized into two completely different projects. The first was a family film, which Monty made with Bill Travers; he and Bill had met during the making of *Born Free*. It was completed in four weeks with everyone working round the clock as near as time and nerves would allow. Producers, directors, stars all had other commitments the moment the month was out; besides, there was the small matter of the budget....

Every day, every requirement and every incident in film making (in Africa anyway) is an emergency. In the end, you come to accept a state of emergency as normal. This little film also had its problems; to begin with, we couldn't find a baby elephant already in captivity. Nor could we have one specially trapped for the purpose because this would have meant violating principles essential to the type of films that Bill Travers and his wife Ginny want to make, and the message they hope to convey in them. Monty called wardens, trappers and veterinary surgeons. Just as the matter was becoming crucial, he procured help from the Kenya Government: they had promised a present of a baby elephant to the London Zoo. It was not due to sail for a month and Monty could have the use of it for the intervening twenty-eight days.

There was still the problem of a suitable location to solve. For several reasons, Monty finally decided that Tsavo East Game Park would be ideal – provided he could get permission from its game warden, David Sheldrick.

Monty has known David for many years, they were in the army together during World War II; but as David has a deep aversion to publicity of any kind, let it suffice to say that he and his wife Daphne belong essentially to the diminishing few whose own personal world suffices them. And their world, in this case, is Tsavo.

Tsavo is far more than a job to David. It is an absorbing interest, a world of plants and trees and insects and animals whose changing cycles he has watched over the years; it is a world of rocks and hills and changing skies and the solitude he enjoys. After all these years of developing it and living so close to it, he has come to regard it as his own domain. He might well have regarded a film unit – however small – as an intrusion, but he was to give us his unstinted co-operation. He was also to allow us to use his tame orphan animals in the film; these animals, combined with a simple little bungalow, were two of the features which made Tsavo East Game Park such a desirable location for this particular picture.

The bungalow was inhabited by Mavis and Philip Huck, farmers who had become amateur botanists. Its two rooms were built of wooden slats, its border gay with flowers that Mavis Huck had lovingly planted. It looked towards a rocky hill, and each of the trees nearby had been identified by the Hucks and neatly labelled with its Latin name. Next to the bungalow stood a truck fitted out like a caravan so that its owners were completely mobile. But next to the truck, in the heart of the bush amongst the thorn trees and the elephants and the rhinos, stood the most delightful incongruity: a highly polished Bentley.

Individualists anyway, this Bentley gave Philip and Mavis Huck a certain dash. Not young any more, they are very active and completely absorbed in their work. They live away from people, but they still like and enjoy them; otherwise they would not have agreed to an intrusion of their privacy for a three week duration by the little film company.

Leaving Monty to discuss the proposition with them, I went off with one of David's game wardens to see the orphans. Six ostrich chicks accompanied us. The size of large hens now, they trooped solemnly behind us along the narrow red path that wound between the bushes and the outcrops of rock. It was hot, and it was very still, the stillness seeming to tremble with that expectancy so typical of the bush.

We came to a pond and there I saw a strange little gathering wallowing in the mud and feeding on a bank: a couple of half-grown buffalo and an ostrich, two half-grown elephant, a full-grown rhino and a baby.

'Be careful of Kadenge,' the game warden said, 'he is still a little wild.'

Kadenge was one of the two elephants, he had simply left the wild herd and attached himself to the orphans. Perhaps he himself was an orphan, and he had wandered into the Game Park from the adjoining hunting block where his parents had been shot. The other elephant was Eleanor (Daphne Sheldrick has written about Eleanor and the other orphans in her book *Orphans of Tsavo*) who grew up in the precincts of the Sheldrick household, stepping with huge-footed delicacy round their daughter when she was a baby crawling on the floor. . . . It seems the furthest possible limit of trust between man and animal.

I went in amongst the orphans to photograph them. The rhino butted me gently in the rear, a buffalo nuzzled my arm . . . it all seemed completely unreal.

Pole Pole, the elephant we had borrowed for the film, was to join this harmonious band. How she would react, and what sort of a reception she would receive, was a matter of some concern.

CIRCLE V

Pole Pole was behaving extremely strangely. We had been told by the trapper that she had been in captivity in the bush for two months, yet when she arrived in Nairobi, the little elephant was so wild and hostile one would have thought that she had been in captivity for only two days. Normally a small animal taken from its parents will grow tame very quickly, especially a baby elephant for it craves constant company and affection. But Pole Pole allowed no one to approach her, waving her trunk at them and charging when they attempted to do so.

Pending her journey to Tsavo, another trapper was taking care of her in Nairobi. Lissa was at school, but Mandy and I used to go and visit her frequently. At five o'clock sharp, the trapper, 'a precise middle-aged gentleman' as Mandy aptly described him, would neatly slice fruit cake and pour tea for us under the tree near his cottage. A twinkle in his blue eyes, he would talk about the days when he used to lasso zebra on horseback, and the Kenya of thirty years ago.

After tea, he would let Mandy enter the run of a young lesser kudu that had captivated her with its soft gaze and velvet flanks and timid ways. Then there were a couple of rhinos that used to fall into a trance while we scratched them under their eyes; for all their cantankerous reputation, rhinos quickly become tame to the point of placidity in captivity.

We would spend the greater part of our time with Pole Pole, offer her succulent leaves through the wooden bars of her compound, or simply stand nearby talking to her. Animals are very susceptible to voice, but the truculent Pole Pole had obviously been badly frightened – we could think of no other reason for her strange behaviour after two months in captivity – and it would take many patient hours to reassure her. We were afraid it might even take long weeks, in which case we would be unable to use her in the film.

Meantime, Pole's co-stars Bill Travers and his wife Virginia McKenna had arrived. During Monty's association with the film industry, a positive result is a few real friends we have made; amongst these number Bill and Ginny Travers. They stayed with us during that first week of filming in Nairobi, but my only recollections of it are early morning departures with Monty and arrivals home after dark at night; of a drink by the fire and dinner and a chat before bed. Happy simply to be back in Africa, Bill and Ginny didn't object to the long hours and hard work. They have a great capacity for work, these two, which is boosted by their enthusiasm.

When the filming in Nairobi was completed, the unit moved down to Tsavo. Bill and Ginny, in preference to the little hotel just outside the game park, chose to live in a one-roomed shack with a veranda nearby the Hucks' cottage. That way, they could be closer to Africa and realize a long cherished desire.

When Ginny was not acting, she was cooking, making beds and washing-up. Bill was revising script material and attending the inevitable production meetings in which the day's problems were discussed or the sequence of the following day's shooting. He needed all his unflagging energy and single-mindedness (which can at times hinder him by its inflexibility) and all his drive and tenacity. It is these traits, combined with an aware intelligence that transform into reality many of the ideas and projects always simmering, sometimes boiling, in his head.

Ginny stands steadfastly behind him. It is extremely difficult to be an actor without being dominated by a demanding ego;

the profession itself demands it. But Ginny is an exception and perhaps because of this she has been able to put her family and her home before her career. I do not associate her with the film world at all; her cottage in England, deep in the Surrey countryside, is a far more fitting back-drop, or the rambling house in Scotland, dreaming in the soft Scottish mists, where I spent a few days with her and Bill during the filming of *Ring of Bright Water*.

It was a far cry from the house in Scotland with its view of loch and hills (whose bewitched remoteness, as a matter of fact, had the same pull on me as some parts of Kenya) to the little shack in the African bush. There is some discrepancy too between elephants and otters.

Pole Pole had joined the unit in Tsavo by now. In the meantime, we had discovered the reason for her strange behaviour: she had not in fact been in captivity for two months before she came to Nairobi, but only for three weeks.

The shock of captivity causes a wild animal to lose weight during the first five weeks. After this time it adapts itself, regains the loss in weight and calms down. The trapper in Nairobi seemed to doubt that we would find her sufficiently amenable to work with, and everyone was extremely concerned.

David Sheldrick had a roomy compound full of succulent leaves ready for her when she arrived at Tsavo and for the first three days, he himself or a couple of his rangers kept her constant company. They coaxed and cajoled her with sugar-cane and oranges and soon she began to respond to their voices and the delicacies they offered her. When finally they let her out of the compound the change was incredible. Almost immediately, she started to follow Ginny around like a child.

Then came the introduction to Eleanor. Very simply, the older elephant put one foreleg protectively round Pole's little body and curled her trunk about her. Pole Pole belonged.

Monty commuted to Voi some of the time during the three weeks that followed, and sometimes I would go with him. One morning of sunlight and breeze before the rocks had yet grown hot and the horizon a hundred miles or so across the bush was still a little misted, we had a ten o'clock rendezvous with the elephants. It was incredible the way David always had them there dead on time – I wish I could be as punctual. The desired shot was one of the animals climbing the red earth path that wound between the rocks until they disappeared from view. It wasn't a very steep incline, but for some reason best known to themselves, and despite all the coaxing from David and the rangers, they refused to co-operate.

Simon had a camera focused on them at one point along the path; Robert Kingston-Davies, the second photographer, had another several yards further on. But every time they walked within shooting distance of the second camera, the animals turned round and walked adamantly back again.

Director James Hill, short, a little stocky, wearing a blue cotton jacket, danced nervously from foot to foot his prematurely white hair gleaming in the sun. Good company and very intelligent, *bon viveur* and musically gifted, as unstintingly generous as he is aware of the value of money, his usually even temper is occasionally interspersed with an unpredictable burst of temperament or temper. A complex, rather secretive character, he delights in the eccentric and the exotic, the beautiful and the bizarre. His interests range from art to old model cars and he prefers, of his own admission, the more selfish existence of a man without the ties and responsibilities of a family. Now here he was in Africa directing a couple of unco-operative elephants in the blazing tropical sun.

Despite the heat, and a fraction of the crew he was accustomed to, he would shoot take after take of the same sequence with a customary exactness and sureness of motive that I enjoyed watching. But the animals would not respond to direction, nor were they moved by impatience; they were not, after all, from a circus.

I thought, as I sat watching in the sun on a rocky ledge above the path, of the elephant in the film *Mr Moses*. She was a circus elephant who had been shipped all the way from South Africa. Her trainer, a small, warm, talkative man, used to speak to her in a mixture (I think) of Hungarian, Afrikaans and Yiddish. 'Suzy mein Bebbily', he would say in the warmest possible tones of enthusiasm and love, 'Suzy mein Bebbily, ist sie brav ist sie *brav*!' But occasionally she was disobedient, and then he would grow angry and scold her. Monty discredits the story (he wasn't there when it happened and I am willing to admit it may have been a coincidence) but one day I saw Suzy cry. Her trainer cursed and shouted at her and great tears fell upon the dusty earth and left a small damp patch as though there had been a little rain....

Eleanor and Pole Pole were too independent of human beings to take much notice of pleadings and threats, but David had his own methods. He fetched some sugar-cane and strewed it along the path and the elephants wandered off in search of it like children gathering wild strawberries.

Watching the little elephant trundle trustfully after Eleanor, it was sad to think that in a week or two she would be taken from the sunlit freedom of the bush, and Eleanor's protective company, to a cage in a London zoo. I remembered how elephants had saddened me as a child during a hated expedition to a circus; so had the clowns, and so had Charlie Chaplin in a film I once saw at a children's party. There is a pathos that the great actor, the elephant and the clown all have in common. It is, I think, the pathos of vulnerability.

*

Within a month of completing *An Elephant called Slowly* Monty and producer Bill Graf began production of the major project. This was a documentary about elephants, and Monty and Simon's original conception of the idea. There were to be no actors, only elephants and other animals, and shooting was to cover the minimum of a year. We all tried for months to think of a suitable name for the film, but we always came back to the simple and self-explanatory title: 'African Elephant'.

Simon and Laila disappeared into the bush. There began a series of weeks and months in which each day started at five so that Simon could catch the beauty of the first light, and ended at eight or nine when he had finished cleaning his cameras and Laila had typed out all his notes.

Monty joined him whenever he could – which was not nearly often enough. Not long ago, we had a rendezvous with him in Tanzania, in the midst of the Serengeti Plains immortalized in Grzimeks' book *Serengeti Shall Not Die*. We were loading the safari car prior to our departure when the phone rang. It was a pilot with a message from Simon to say the road was mudbound, we should cross into Tanzania by an alternative route. What we did not know was that Simon had later given a second pilot a further message to say the rain was everywhere and we should not come at all.

We got up early – too early; four o'clock in the morning is a

CIRCLE V

time to end a day, not to begin it. But we had three hundred miles of road to traverse, the conditions were uncertain, and we would have to make camp when we arrived at our destination.

It is only a hundred miles to the Kenya Tanzania border by the route that we took, and it is a further seventy miles from the border to the sleepy little town of Arusha. The road that leads to it winds through a clutch of green and gold hills, territory of the brilliantly cloaked Warush who are cousins of the Masai. Another seventy miles and we passed Lake Manyara, famous for its elephants.

We didn't stop at the lake this time but drove straight on, climbing an earth road that was both slippery and corrugated: we had finally hit the storm. Soon we were up in the forests, green fungus trailing from trees secreted by the veils of rain. As we ascended a side of the famous Ngorongoro Crater Monty kept saying: 'You must see the view, you simply have to see the view'. Both he and Mandy had been here before but I had never been beyond the lake. All I could see, however, was the driving rain and the cloud, cloud was rolling out of the mouth of the crater like thick smoke from a chimney pot. We began to descend the other side of the crater – had I not been told it was there, I would have passed it by without even knowing that a few yards from where we were driving the earth suddenly dropped a couple of thousand feet like some gigantic well.

The road deteriorated into a muddy track. When the cloud lifted momentarily, I could see that we were driving through a scene of great beauty; hills winged away from us in wide green curves, then gentled at their foot into a generous sweep of wide green plain – everything was green, verdant and fresh as

Ireland, only you couldn't mistake where you were because of the breadth of dimension, the unstinted scale of it all.

The hills began easing themselves into an enormous plain. It stretched to the horizon in every direction and nowhere was it relieved by either bush or hummock or tree; it was in fact a grass desert. This was the beginning of Serengeti. But only the beginning, for Serengeti covers an area of five and a half thousand square miles.

There were thousands of plains game, never had we seen so many. Their numbers were so great that from the distance they looked like stones scattered across the grass.

We were witnessing the great annual migration of zebra and wildebeest.

I do not believe that Lissa's and Mandy's children will see such a sight and the scene had a certain poignancy because I was aware of its transience. The animals continued appearing, more and still more of them, great winding columns, which were sometimes six and seven miles long, six and ten abreast. They were moving off in search of fresh pastures (usually more water too, but now the rain had come) and they knew where they were going; yet they looked lost, wandering like refugees who had been driven by the enemy from their town. It wasn't until afterwards that it struck me how apt the simile might one day become.

The entrance to the Park itself is marked by a barrier across the road where you must stop and show the pass previously purchased in order to enter. We knew that Simon had not yet arrived, because it is also necessary to sign the ranger's book, and Simon's signature was not amongst the two or three scrawled beneath that day's entries.

Our meeting place was ten miles away, at Lake Lagarjia.

CIRCLE V

Monty thought Simon might just have made his way there by some alternative route, and we headed down the track to the lake. Here the terrain was semi-waterlogged. Twice we skidded in a circle and once we landed in the middle of a thick bush that obligingly gave way and keeled over.

We came to the lake; it was quite small, less than half a mile in length perhaps, and surrounded by trees. There was no sign of a tent amongst them, nor could we find any wheel tracks in the sodden earth. When Monty stopped the vehicle and climbed out to look around, we were immediately inundated with lake flies. The soil was black cotton and sticky as sand; another shower of rain and we would never be able to leave the lake, even in low ratio four-wheel drive.

We turned back and drove the ten miles to the game ranger's post, stationed right at the foot of the knoll; it was the only elevation in the land we had seen since we entered the plain. The game ranger gave us permission to make camp in the shelter of the hillock. 'Be careful of the snakes,' he called after us. 'There are lots of spitting cobras you know.'

We didn't. Mandy and I were all for spending the night in the safari car. It wasn't so much the snakes as laziness: it seemed hardly worth putting up a complicated tent just for one night. Besides, it had already grown dark. But Monty was all for a little comfort and a decent night's rest.

There were lions as well as snakes. They growled continuously and a little too close for comfort the entire time we were putting up the tent: I remembered Simon telling us to treat the Serengeti lions with the greatest respect....

That night the canvas flapped in the violent gusts of wind like the sails of a ship in a storm, and the rain beat down continuously. Mandy and I were so tired we slept through most of it, but Monty lay awake listening. How glad we were that we had not stayed at Lake Lagarjia; we might have been marooned there for days.

In the morning, we drove the thirty miles across the plain to Seronera Lodge which Simon would have to pass were he travelling via Keekorok. The swollen clouds were so close to earth it felt as though at any moment they might press down upon our heads, then it began to rain again, the heavy grey skein of water fusing heaven and earth. We watched the plains of Serengeti turn slowly into a lake.

By a strange coincidence, we arrived at Seronera Lodge at the same moment as Simon and Laila. They were very surprised to see us, until we explained that we had not received their second message. The bridge just beyond Keekorok had been under water and they had had to wait until it subsided in order to cross; on account of the heavy rain everywhere they had changed their plans and were going to film in the Ngorongoro Crater. I of course was delighted: I would see it after all.

It cleared as we began leaving the plain and climbing into the hills once more, there was a fresh breeze blowing and the promise of a fine evening. Finally we drew near the edge of the crater. Its rim was clearly delineated in the soft evening light as though it had been stencilled, and symmetrical enough to have been drawn by a gigantic compass; two thousand feet below, cupped in the heart of a green circle of hills and bordered by grassland, a quiet lake reflected pale gold clouds in a hushed sky. The hills were steep, yet there was nothing angular about them; they were all curves and pleats and folds and everywhere, after the rain, it was green.

We began the descent into the crater. There is a notice at the top 'Four-wheel drive only', and it is not there for decoration.

CIRCLE V

The track winds steeply down the precipice it has been hewn from; the rock face towers vertical as a wall on one side, and there is a sheer drop into the crater on the other. The wheels just manage to grip the loose earth and bump uneasily over the projections of rock. Below, the sunlit water and the grass lie dreaming in the deep green hollow of the hills. As we descended lower the dark specks scattered across the grassland took on the form of wildebeest and Thompson's gazelles; almost every female had a baby at its side and the grass was scattered with bouquets of white flowers. It was almost too much, a page out of a children's story-book: *Heidi* perhaps.

We drove a little way round the water then left the lake and headed into a glade of fever trees caught in the last rays of sunlight. When the sun catches the barks and branches of these thorn trees they are lit with a lambent golden glow; this, combined with the delicacy of their shape and the fine tracery of leaves produces an incredibly beautiful interplay of form, texture and light.

We made camp beyond the glade beneath two great fig trees that stood at the foot of a steep, wooded hill. The setting was perfect. We could see the lake and twelve miles away, on the other side, a part of the girder of hills. There were scattered trees between us and the water, and the great fig trees with their knotted barks spread wide branches across our tents. The knots are formed by a parasite of smooth bark, hard as iron, that clamps itself to the bole and winds itself round it. Eventually, Kamau once told me, it will strangle the tree.

We could hear the deep, bass bleat of the vociferous wildebeest and the occasional squeal of a zebra. Simon warned us to take everything into our tents before we went to bed, for the hyena in the district are wildly voracious and there is nothing which they will not eat. Last time he was here with a white hunter and his clients, the hyena chewed right through a safari box (a stout wooden crate) and ate twelve dozen eggs just flown in. He and the white hunter slept through the entire orgy but the client slept not a wink. In the morning, chewed and bent saucepans were scattered far and wide, tins of bully beef had had the meat sucked out of them and the alarm clock was bent – Simon leant awkwardly to one side imitating the angle and grinned – but it still works nevertheless. If the hyena left us alone, it would be because the wildebeest were calving and the hyena were lurking nearby, ready to seize the babies at birth.

Morning brought a ruff of pink clouds resting lightly on the rim of the crater on one side, a red sun rising on the other; zebra scattered round our tents, the honey-bird calling *ki-fa-ro*, *ki-fa-ro* (rhino, rhino) and the high, silvery note of the African kite.

We drove off, in search of a birth sequence for the film. Up hill and down dale we went, across slopes that ran free and wild and green. Great purple clouds gathered and it began to rain. Ahead of us, Simon's vehicle nosed dramatically skywards, then dived into a valley again dotted with wildebeest.

That evening it was fine once more and when we returned the sun was setting behind the rim of the crater. A few pink flamingoes were standing in the shallow water by the lake edge, and a fine herd of powerful eland. Wildebeest were galloping across the grass, spirited foals at their side; they are able to run with their mothers barely more than twenty minutes after their birth. It is just as well they can, or they would all fall easy prey to the predators.

CIRCLE V

Back at camp, while Laila cooked dinner and Mandy wrote her diary (an enormous ledger filled with thousands of lines of minute handwriting, photographs and cuttings), Monty and Simon discussed *African Elephant*.

Many elephant sequences were to be shot at Lake Manyara, where we joined Simon on another occasion. We didn't take our tents this time but stayed in a little round thatched hut temporarily vacated by the scientist studying the Manyara herds. The hut stands on the edge of a rocky drop a short distance up a rocky escarpment. The craggy cliff-face is patched with bushes and thorn trees and baobabs, while below the rondavel a waterfall cascades down a narrow gully that cuts between the rocks. It makes a sound like wind rushing through trees and empties into a shallow river whose bed is tumbled with great, rough hewn hunks of rock that are buff, grey and sandy-pink.

There is a place on the river not far from this point where the water is deeper and it slips in runnels with a soft splashing sound over the rocks. Here we watched baboons playing with Thompson gazelles (these animals often keep one another company) and a pied kingfisher fluttering above the water, till it swooped suddenly on its prey. Then elephants came down to drink, many babies amongst them. One of them was wearing a transmitting collar, fitted by tranquillizing the animal with darts; receivers pick up the transmissions and it is thus possible to keep track of the elephant's movements.

Elephants, like people, manifest different characteristics individually and different characteristics in general according to the location. At Manyara they are used to tourists, and if you know what you are doing it is possible to go in amongst a herd. Even so, one cantankerous female resented Simon's frequent intrusion; she would flap her ears and trumpet and threaten to charge – and occasionally did. On one occasion she picked up a log of wood and hurled it on the roof of his vehicle.

We were deep amongst the elephants at Manyara, sometimes right in amongst a herd. Due to the film, I have had the opportunity of learning many intriguing facts about their habits, several of which have only been discovered in the last five years, because Monty has access to the latest findings of game wardens and scientists.

It is the elephant who is the uncontested king of beasts. When he appears at a water-hole, even rhino and buffalo will move away; as for the lion, he walks past them as though they do not exist. In Manyara Game Park, the lions sleep in the trees, perhaps for reasons of safety; although they have little to fear from the elephants who at worst may trample a cub to death, possibly in protest or revenge, because lions will seize a baby elephant and feed on him if they get the chance.

There is in fact a story of a lion who killed an elephant calf; the elephant, in revenge, tracked down the lion's cub and trampled it to death. She then lifted it up and carried it to where her dead calf lay, laid it down beside her own calf and covered the two of them with grass and twigs.

It is quite customary for elephants to bury their dead in this fashion, and they even buried an unconscious African woman on one occasion. I had heard the story before, but Terence Adamson told me it first hand, at Kora Hill. It seems that one of his workers was returning home when he heard faint cries. Following the direction they emanated from, the man found a pile of grass and twigs deposited by elephants – and beneath it, the woman, quite unharmed if a little short of air. . . .

CIRCLE V

Terence told me too of the elephant that fell down a well at Marsabit; how he and his workers had filled the well with stones, the elephant shuffling his feet with each fresh load until it was sufficiently high up to climb out; how it had regarded him quietly from the other side of the well as though recognizing his debt, instead of racing away to freedom or even attacking his liberator as another animal might have done. 'I thought he was going to come up and shake hands,' Terence said, 'I had to shoo him away so that my workers would go back to the well and start taking out the stones. He walked about five yards off, then stood waiting. So I had to shoo him off again, but he wouldn't go further than ten yards and just stood there quietly feeding.'

There was a woman who lived in Tanzania on a farm (it is now Momella Game Lodge) who is said to have consorted with elephants very much like Terence Adamson. She would walk in the forest amongst them unharmed, and when she died, they surrounded her house, trunks in the air, just as they surround a baby elephant when it is born. George Adamson, in his autobiography, maintains that they have 'an abstract idea of death.'

There are no elephant graveyards, though. The myth probably occurred because African hunters used to light a circle of fire round a herd in order to make a mass killing, or because old elephants prefer to remain close to marshy places because the grass is damp and needs less chewing so that several skeletons may thus be found in one area. Elephants have a strange inexplicable habit of playing with the bones of their dead, and one of pulling out the tusks, carrying them off, and hiding them elsewhere. This story is usually discredited (a well-known American magazine turned it down) but David

Sheldrick has seen it – and Simon actually managed to photograph the sequence for the film.

When an elephant has lost his last set of teeth (he has six in all) or they have grown too worn to chew, a young bull will often keep fierce guard over him. Elephants show a responsibility towards one another that goes far beyond the protection of a cow or a calf; they have been seen, like dolphins, supporting a wounded comrade on either side and hurrying him out of danger; they have been seen feeding a member of the herd whose trunk has been injured so that he could not feed himself. And although they normally ignore the other animals, two bull elephants were once found guiding and protecting a blind buffalo.

Usually the only intruders they suffer are egrets and piacpiacs who eat the insects disturbed by the elephant's feet as he walks. Whilst the birds are eating the insects, the elephant is feeding on a variety of grasses and leaves. He also has a weakness for black plums and desert dates, wild figs and raspberries, olives and celery and ginger; one would not give so ponderous a creature credit for such delicate tastes, nor imagine that he would be so discriminating. He knows by scent which plant to eat and which to leave. He can strip the tiniest leaf from a branch with his trunk, he can wrap it round clumps of grass, and he can pick up seeds shaken from fruit and pods. His appetite is more in keeping with his size: he consumes an average of three hundred pounds of food a day and drinks, when it is available, between thirty and fifty gallons of water.

When he drinks, he sucks the water into his trunk and then blows it into his mouth and down his throat. The babies just use their mouths and often lie on their sides in the water to do this. Sometimes, after he has been chased by his only enemy,

CIRCLE V

Man, he will squirt water over his back, drawing it perhaps from a special compartment in his stomach.

In the dry season, he will dig with his feet in a dried up river bed and wait for the water to rise and settle; he shows great patience and self-discipline in this, for he has sometimes journeyed many miles and is very thirsty. If the calves try to drink before the water has settled, the cows hold them back, then, when it is time, they quench their thirst in an established hierarchy: the matriarch first, the smallest calf last of all. Sometimes, before leaving, they plug the hole with chewed bark or a ball of grass and leaves; the African game rangers say this is to stop the other animals from drinking at the pool, and quite possibly it is true.

Elephants are inordinately fond of water. They bathe every day if they can and we have often watched them playing in a river, splashing and rolling; frequently the only visible part of a small calf is his trunk. They may be very noisy in the water, drinking or at play, but on land they can move with a silence that is uncanny. Elastic-like pads on their feet aid this. There is no crashing through the bush either, nothing more than the snap of a twig so that at night they seem to pass as shadows, and it is quite haunting.

They are unrestrainedly vociferous when they want to be – on land as well as in the water, so much so it has even been claimed (perhaps by a misogynist) that this is the reason a herd is usually accompanied by only one mature bull while the others keep away. The mothers and the calves are nervous, and if a cow is not screaming at a wayward calf, she is calling to him with a deep, prolonged rumbling which for so long was thought to come not from the vocal chords but the stomach. When she charges, she trumpets furiously, and she also uses the rumbling tones to inform the rest of the herd of her whereabouts.

Whether they object to the noise or no, the male progeny are forcibly ejected by her when they reach puberty: perhaps it is because they are sometimes too rough with the smaller members of the family. For a while, they are a little lost and bewildered but then they meet up with other young males similarly exiled and begin to enjoy life again. The association they form with these bulls is quite loose, as opposed to the close knit matriarchal family unit, but very amicable; elephants are essentially pacifist and rarely fight. Before they are fully grown, the males engage in test battles to gauge their strength and according to the results, establish a hierarchy amongst themselves similar to that of the females. This dictates their behaviour at water-holes and also perhaps in the presence of a female in season, for even in these circumstances it is unusual for two bulls to do battle.

Elephants are unusually adaptable to climate, and if they are most numerous at Tsavo, in the regions of the fifth circle, they also bathe in the sea at the coast, inhabit low areas of hot, dusty bush – and roam ten thousand feet high in the foothills of mountain ranges with hoar frost clinging to their stalwart frames. . . . This capacity to adapt themselves – to food as well as climate – is yet another characteristic that singles them out from other animals.

We have come to a time of terrible dilemma over the elephant. Are the areas left to the herds large enough to support them? Must we cull several thousand, as at Murchison Falls in Uganda, in order to protect the health of those that remain? The health of elephants depend on their numbers and the fertility of the habitat which they occupy. In order to discover

CIRCLE V

whether the herds in Tsavo National Park were healthy or unhealthy, increasing or decreasing, the scientist responsible for the research concluded that it was necessary to crop three thousand elephant. From the carcasses he would be able to obtain immediate answers to urgent questions.

Arguments raged for and against, none more prolonged or heated than between Monty and Peter Beard. Peter was for culling and had taken part in the pilot scheme which necessitated the cropping of three hundred elephant: Monty was against.

Frequently people who argue against culling are sentimentalists – with elephant, it is difficult not to be. But Monty maintains that if we studied the habitat first, it may be that the cropping would prove unnecessary. It is not yet known how much land, and of what type, is necessary to support a herd of a given number. The answer lies in the habitat as well as in the carcasses of the dead animals. But how much time have we for this method?

It is true that elephant are frequently destructive in their eating habits. They will push over small trees, eat a few leaves and wander on; they will strip large trees of their bark (they are especially fond of baobabs) ringing them in the process so that the tree eventually dies. But Monty and I have seen areas denuded of trees by the elephant covered with a profusion of grass and bushes only a few years later. It is probable that this terrain with its new type of vegetation can now support more animals than before. We also noticed in one area where saplings were springing up to replace dead trees that the elephants seem to leave the young trees alone and concentrate on the grass. There is also a theory that many trees thought to have been killed by the elephant have in fact died for other reasons.

Be that as it may, the authorities decided against culling.

But the problem will soon rise again. Africa is vast, yet even here there has been a population explosion and land where the elephant once roamed freely is now under cultivation. Every day Man encroaches a little more on territory which once belonged to the animals, and the time has already come when he is squeezing the elephant out.

CIRCLE VI

Baharini

AT some point where the sun-steeped reaches of the sixth circle meet the deserted white sands and lapis lazuli fringe of the Indian ocean, there stands a small blue and white bungalow on a cliff-top suspended between sky and sea.

It is wide open to the clouds and the ocean and full of breeze and sunlight. The windows are framed with blue wood, unrestricted by curtains or glass so that looking through them at the sea and the golden tree on the cliff edge is like viewing an Old Master's painting in a blue frame. Life here slips by rather like a dream. Time has no significance, we eat when we are hungry and sleep when we are sleepy, only the bells mark the divisions in the day. The breeze carries them clearly across the creek to us for this bungalow faces partly across an inlet and partly on to the ocean itself. The breeze carries the voice of the muezzin as well, his hoarse cry so fortified with zeal he might be calling Allah's praise from the roof of our little cottage instead of standing high in the minaret of his white mosque across the water. We were warned that his first zealous exhortations would boom across the creek at five fifteen – why five fifteen we complained that first morning, woken from sleep and not yet accustomed to the sound, why not six, isn't that the time he's supposed to waken all good Muslims for prayer? Perhaps we were muddling it with Mass.

The little cottage is cool and quiet and the little cove at the foot of the cliff deserted; no one comes near but the man with the fish. At high tide the cove is completely cut off, but when the sea ebbs one can walk along the winding shore. There is a coral bed full of tiny pools that flash with colour and life, and behind the coral reef, on the cliff top, grow great girthed baobab trees. The coastal tribes say that good spirits live in trees, except for these baobabs which are haunted and harbour the devils that witch-doctors have exorcised from men. They say too that the devil planted the baobab upside down, and it is undeniable that when the branches are not in leaf they look like twisted roots. The cavernous hollows are full of bats; hornbills, red-breasted barbets and buffalo weavers make their homes in its ample branches. Fruit-bats and bush babies will awaken with the moonlight (Mitzy's origin was probably in one of these havens) and in season, exotic white flowers will bloom for twenty-four hours; the bush babies and the fruit-bats pollinate them.

There is a tribe in Kenya, almost extinct today, called the Wanderobo, who some believe might be the descendants of the original bushmen. Wanderers without homes, they spend their days hunting elephant for food and gathering wild honey which the bees make in the secret hollows of the baobabs. Today, elephant hunting is permitted only with a licence, so that the few Wanderobo who remain – and the vanishing Liangulu, or 'Elephant People' as they are often called – are labelled poachers with the rest. How, one wonders, do they reconcile their own punishment for killing in order to obtain traditional food, with the white hunter's prerogative for sport? But honey remains any man's prize who cares to risk the vicious stings of Africa's fierce bees, and the honey-bird will lead him to the treasure. It will flit from tree to tree chirruping to his human companions and waiting for them to catch him up. Then, the hive located, the men light a fire and burn elephant dung to sedate the bees with the smoke whilst they steal the combs. One of these they always pin on a thorn of a nearby tree for their little guide (the baobab has no thorns) and legend has it that if they forget this small token of gratitude a curse will be laid upon them for their churlishness.

Honey for men and for birds, pollen for bush babies and fruit-bats, refuge for a thousand living things, the great green pods of the baobab hang down over the cliff edge and finally drop on to the sand near the coral pools. Tiny tropical fish, each of them a different shape and shade, many of them iridescent blues and greens dart to and fro in the limpid water of the hollowed rocks. Sea snakes slide to safety at our approach, the soft insidiousness of their movements like poured oil, while a sea slug lies obese and still amongst the starfish and the shells and the pastel coloured stones.

In our garden above the cove there are many birds and frequently swallows fly straight through the house. Hawks often circle the lawn and two green and yellow parakeets perch in the tree on the cliff edge. There is a little bench on the edge of the cliff which, bushes and creepers entangled in its rocks, drops sheer beneath without wall or fence – not the best place for Lissa to dream her dreams, I thought. But in the end it was Amanda who gave us the fright, perched on that precarious plank.

Lissa and I were lying lazily on chaise longues, reading. Mandy was convoluted on the cliff bench in one of those unlikely attitudes she usually assumes as long as she is not forced to sit at a desk at school. Suddenly: 'Look at that hawk!' Lissa exclaimed. Poised on the branch of a tree, wings outspread, strangely still and intent, a hawk was waiting to drop with deadly swiftness on its prey. It rose into the air, then sank straight down with a ruthless purpose of motion as fast and steady as a stone in water – and hovered within half an inch of Amanda's head. Mesmerized, I recalled the story of an acquaintance at Mombasa who used to toss lumps of meat into the air for the hawks until finally they grew so tame they would swoop down and take the food from her hand. But one day a bird clawed her cheek, gouging it viciously. The hawk was above Mandy's head, the cliff beneath her feet. Engrossed in her book, for a moment or two Amanda was unaware of the winged monster. Then suddenly she yelled, and leapt into the air – not quite over the cliff-top but quite near enough! – and the bird flew off.

Every night since the girls and I have been here, a bright ripple of water like a silver chain has roped this side of the creek to the other. We like to sit on the bench and watch the moonlit sea of an evening or the boats sailing past by day. The dhows fascinate us especially: Arab dhows, their sails spread to the wind, their hold filled with copra and ivory and spice, heading, as they have done for centuries, for the Red Sea and the Persian Gulf; African dhows, or 'sewn-boats', made by the Bajun fishermen from mangrove poles laced together without a single nail, just as they were made two thousand years ago.

The Bajun village of Waitamu lies about thirty miles up the coast from the bungalow in which we are staying. The road that leads to it burrows deep in sand between baobabs and palms, kapok and cashew nut trees. Men file past in bright *kikois* and women in the short, bulky skirts peculiar to the coast; they

CIRCLE VI

carry bulging sacks of cotton and the cotton spills over the top like white candy floss.

The village itself is hidden away amongst a grove of coconut trees overlooking Blue Lagoon. There are a few Swahili and even a couple of Ethiopians among the villagers, but they are all Muslims. In the centre of the thatched huts and the palms stands a small white mosque; I went in once. An African drew a pail of water from the stone bath in the entrance hall and threw it over my feet; one must be clean to worship Allah. Inside it was cool and white and an old man mumbled a blessing into his long grey beard, or perhaps it was a verse from the Koran.

And once – I cannot think what possessed me for I hate to sew – I took it into my head to teach these Bajun ladies embroidery, of all things. They liked the coloured threads and the novelty of the occupation, and I liked watching them cook or listening to their tales in the little courtyards round which their huts are built, Arab style. There was always a low stool in these courtyards with a sharp knife projecting from one end; sitting astride the stool, the women would grate coconuts against this blade. Then they put the shredded nut into cylindrical bags of plaited palm fronds, squeezing and twisting them to extract the coconut juice in which they subsequently cooked the rice.

Beyond the palm grove *ngalawas* lie beached in Blue Lagoon. Sometimes we go out to the reef with one of the fishermen in the narrow, hollowed craft of rough wood, bobbing serenely over the turquoise water that sifts the pale, clean sand below. The fisherman lends us cotton handlines with stone sinkers, but fishing to me is incidental; I am happy simply to be back by the sea.

When we near the reef we put on our goggles and climb into

the water – and a world of filtered sunshine and secret depths, a world of fantastic rocks and twisted coral and trailing plants and shoals of fish richly coloured as tropical butterflies: a dream-world – which threatens at any moment to turn into a nightmare, transformed by the appearance of a sharp-toothed swordfish or shark. It is said there are none on the shoreward side of the reef, but I have never been fully convinced.

For the Bajun, fishing is a way of life. They know the winds, they know the tides, they know the currents, they know the stars, and for generations the sea has been in their blood. Most of them live on the offshore islands of Kenya, north of the island of Lamu with its sixty mosques, its narrow streets and great white sand dunes. I once spent a couple of days at Lamu in the only 'hotel' it then boasted (today there is one more). The entrance was in a narrow alley, up a dim, narrow, steep flight of stairs. Swallows had nested in the rafters of my bedroom, and the servant placed on the little table a vase of dusty plastic flowers. The sitting-room and dining-room consisted of a veranda which overlooked the waterfront – and the life of the little town. This veranda had a great appeal for me; sitting there, one could feel the rhythm of the island, slow, lazy, unchanged for centuries. Boats glided by with full sail, Arab and Bajun; Arabs, Bajun and Swahilis in coloured *kikois* and little skull caps sat chatting on the waterfront wall, women in purdah flitted by like bats. A thousand swallows wheeled and cried, Indian music wailed, outboard engines droned, and there was the soft plash of water against the wall like a continuous lullaby. At night, a single lantern lit the veranda, geckos scurried across the walls and the wind softly rustled the leaves of the cashew nut tree below. A solitary lantern lit the waterfront at this juncture too, and occasionally a boat would sail into the orbit of the light – then disappear into the blackness like a firefly.

On the wharf of the little harbour where dhows lay waiting for the change of the monsoon, great bundles of mangrove poles were stacked which the Bajun had cut on their nearby islands (or on the mainland) and transported to Lamu for sale. It is an alternative occupation to catching turtles and their main occupation, fishing. They spear the fish, or catch it in the weirs, or in basket traps of palm rib and split bamboo; sometimes they fish at night but then they risk the three-legged ghosts who troop down to the sea to bathe after dark, turning the water blood red. If a Bajun fisherman fails to return, his friends know that he has looked into the face of a ghost and met his death.

Close to the Bajun village of Waitamu on the mainland, facing the bay which adjoins Blue Lagoon, there is a little white-washed shack with arches that open out to the wind and the sea. There is a little wooden bar inside, two or three tables, a collection of cowrie shells and a fishing net spread across one wall; it is here the handful of holiday-makers gather of an evening for a drink or a chat – or used to before there were any hotels.

The bar belonged to Ian Pritchard. He used to take people goggling and water-skiing, and he was the best water-skier and underwater diver in the country. Then one day he hit a piece of coral while skiing in shallow water and broke his neck. He was completely paralysed. Some months later his fiancée Dulcie drove the eight hundred miles from Rhodesia, where she was teaching, to marry him. Now it was Dulcie who ran the bar, looked after the boats and took people fishing and water-skiing and goggling. Last time we were there, there was a little

Frenchman who never wore anything but the briefest triangle of white satin on his small, muscular, copper brown body; an English artist living with her two children in a little makuturoofed shack by the sea; an Irish doctor and his family; a white hunter and a tall Canadian actor who had come for a week and stayed for a year. The first time I saw him I thought he had a pigtail, but he was carrying Ian Pritchard's monkey on his shoulder and its tail was hanging down his back.

Blue-eyed, slight, her blonde hair tied back in a pony tail, with her inexhaustible energy Dulcie managed to find the time and the money to build Ian a studio. If before his world had been the ocean, now it was the realms of art. Whenever we go to Waitamu, we know that we will find Ian sitting in his wheelchair painting, holding the brush in his mouth.

The studio is full of sea and light and Ian's personality. A tall, pleasant-looking man with warm, light brown eyes and a beard (one small boy thought he was Jesus Christ!) he has gentleness and compassion, an unfailing sense of humour – and tremendous determination. If there are people who go to visit him out of pity and thinking to give, they leave with wonder and they take something away. Talking to him (and there is so much to talk about the hours slip away) realizing that he has become entirely independent of his body and learnt to channel his entire energy into the growth of his mind, I wonder constantly at the tremendous inner struggle this man must have fought. Ian himself insists it was sheer contrariness, he has often gained his greatest successes simply because he has been told that failure is inevitable. I find myself thinking of a line of W. H. Auden's as well: 'Most desires end up in stinking ponds.' The opposite must also hold true, and Ian's is the most triumphant of reversals.

CIRCLE VI

The girls and I look through his paintings. The early ones are all of his beloved sea and the clouds, or of the fish that inhabit the underwater world where he once spent so much of his time. Later efforts, as he begins to exploit his talent, cover a diverse range of subjects and styles – we recognize a portrait in which he has caught a vivid expression and an incredible likeness. He asks the African orderly to fetch him another tube of paint (for once the monkey is not meddling with them), and we leave him to work in his peaceful studio with its great vista of the sea.

*

Across the creek sleeps the village of Kilifi. We cross on the ferryboat when we need to replenish our food stocks from the dim little store, or to buy mangoes and pineapples or sweet green bananas from the market. Pawpaws grow in the garden and fish is brought to us daily, often still alive and squirming in the straw basket, so that a trip to Mombasa is in no way essential. But we enjoy rummaging in the little shops and wandering through the old part of the town.

The thirty miles from Kilifi to Mombasa, and the three hundred from Mombasa to Nairobi, are now macadamized. Formerly the road was so bad we often travelled by rail. We used to enjoy this journey in the train, the arrival of the attendant with mattresses and fresh linen to make up our beds; dinner in the restaurant car. There are certain circumstances or stimuli that evoke the same response as they did when one was a child. For me, one of these is eating and sleeping in a train. Lissa and Mandy sleep through the dozens of stops (even today the train takes fourteen hours to cover the three hundred miles – one can do it in five by car) while I consume enough wine to ensure the journey feels as though I am swinging gently through the night on a hammock. A vague consciousness of rumbling wheels sustains a blissful awareness that I am travelling and will awake *baharini*, by the sea.

By rail or by car, one must cross a bridge to enter the port, for Mombasa is an island. In the old days, it used to be called Mvita, Swahili for war, and legend has it that in the thirteenth century it was founded by a man called Shehe Mvita. One day, the story goes, three men told Shehe Mvita that he should dig wells and build mosques of stones. Mvita replied that he would be very happy to do this but he had no lime. Whereupon each of the three men opened up a little box, and lo and behold, they contained lime. I suppose they must have been magic boxes, for like the coin in the fairy-tale purse or the oil jar in the temple, they kept replenishing themselves, and there was sufficient lime to build a mosque. The city grew and prospered, and a Portuguese wrote of it at the beginning of the sixteenth century:

Close to the mainland there is another island which the Moors call Mombaza, very large and beautiful, and full of high and handsome houses of stone and white-wash, and with very good streets in the manner of Quiloa, and it also had a king over it. The people are of dusky and white and brown complexions, and likewise the women, who are much adorned with silk and gold stuffs. It is a town of great trade in goods and it has a port, where there are always many ships, both of those that sail for Sofala, and those that come from Cambay and Melinde [Malindi].... This Mombaza is a country well supplied with plenty of provisions, very fine sheep which have round tails, many cows, chickens, and very large goats, much rice and millet and plenty of oranges, sweet and bitter. Indian figs and all sorts of vegetables and very good water.

CIRCLE VI

'High and handsome' are comparative terms, but there are still some old, double-storey buildings with wooden balconies and faded blue or pink façades lining the narrow streets of the old part of the town. There are dusky women in gold-threaded saris too – and an abundance of sweet oranges and tropical fruits. The girls and I pick our way between colourful mounds of mangoes and bread-fruit, coconuts and custard apples, pommadores and pineapples, bananas, lychees, grenadillas and pawpaw. The little shops that open out on to the street are crammed with rolls of bright cottons and bulging sacks of onions and sesame seeds and spice – nutmeg, cloves, fresh vanilla, cinnamon. Dark-eyed children chase one another between the stalls and hand-carts that block the narrow streets, or stop to gaze hungrily at the piles of oily, Oriental sweet-meats. We can smell incense and cloves, fermented dates and curry, while the thin, high notes of Eastern music weave themselves into the smells and the heat. We arrive, eventually, at the old port.

On the steep, cobbled ascent between the harbour wall and the warehouses, turbanned Indian Sikhs and Arab merchants bargain and speculate in groups of twos and threes. Strong Swahilis, their bodies gleaming in the sun, hump heavy loads from warehouse to longboats; others, chanting monotonously, swing the bulky packages from man to man in a sweating human chain. A few dhows are patiently awaiting their cargoes of ivory and sugar, silver and copra and spice. No one knows exactly how old are the ports of Mombasa and Malindi, Lamu and Zanzibar, but there are some who say that the Egyptian pharaohs and King Solomon knew of them, and that intrepid sailors carried away tortoise shell and gold to adorn the sloe-eyed women of antiquity.

AFRICAN HARVEST

This morning, shortly after dawn, three dhows sailed by; their sails in the early morning light like frail wings blown against a mother of pearl sky, but in the dream-like serenity of their wake they dragged memories of a cruel and flamboyant past in which pirates and cannibals, soldiers and explorers, traders and slaves all played their violent or miserable parts. From the time of Vasco da Gama until the beginning of the last century when the Arabs finally won the day and asked the British for protection, the Portuguese and the Arabs fought for control of the coast. But trade was brisk – and none brisker than the export of slaves.

By many accounts, the Arabs treated their slaves humanely, and even as equals or a part of the family, considering their purchase in terms of 'a portion of a man's work' rather than the man himself, but by all accounts the journey by dhow was appalling. Many of the prisoners died from suffocation or disease and even as a passenger the journey was far from pleasant. The explorer Joseph Thompson wrote in the last century:

A single mast fifteen feet high supports an unwieldy lateen sail of dimensions enormous compared to the size of the craft and held together by rotten coconut fibres which not infrequently startle the crew and the passengers – if they do not do worse – by breaking and letting their whole burden break and crash down on deck. The water leaks in at innumerable points, continually requiring several men to bale night and day. Then, from stem to stern, there rises a combination of smells truly sickening. The rotting wood, with its coating of coconut oil, the accumulated grease and filth of years, the bilge water, the contents of the cargo and the effluvia from the perspiring skins of the negroes all contribute their quota to an effect which words cannot describe.

CIRCLE VI

I went on a dhow once, during the two weeks I spent at Zanzibar. As I was rowed across from the island's sleepy little wharf, I began to feel distinctly nervous. There were several dhows at anchor and on their decks stood the Arab crews, cut-throat rogues in filthy tatters who watched my approach with evil, cunning eyes and villainous grins. But the African oarsman, to my relief, steered me past them and stopped at a boat where no one but the captain was aboard, a polite, softly spoken young man of grave charm. He showed me around the dhow; it was little more than a wooden hulk awaiting its cargo. There was the tall mast and the sail described by Thompson, and the crew still slept on their prayer mats. With customary Arab hospitality, my host offered me dates piled high on an enormous circular copper tray and black coffee which he poured from a copper jug into tiny handleless cups.

Impossible to watch the dhows and not to think of Zanzibar and the two weeks I spent there – just before the arrival of the Chinese and the East Germans; before the island had even had a political coup and politics aroused less reaction than the scent of cloves. The last innovation must have been when they put a stop to the slave trade – and the island's prosperity at the same time.

I went to Zanzibar by boat. It seemed a far more fitting approach to an island with a name as Oriental, as fictitious and as ancient as Zan A'l Bar, Zanzibar, Fair of the Land. It didn't even occur to me to take my passport; the island I thought was part of Kenya and I couldn't imagine anyone bothering with such tiresome products of modern bureaucracy anyway in a region oblivious to change and time.

I climbed the gangplank to begin my romantic journey. It must have been a hundred and ten in the shade, a brass band was playing airs from *The Fellowship Songbook*, the passengers were unattractive, and the food in the sweltering dining-room appalling. I comforted myself with thoughts of Thompson's voyage by dhow and retired to my cabin with an ice cold bottle of wine.

Dusk had fallen by the time we reached the Emerald Isle the following evening. Two phlegmatic Zanzibaree officials with cat-like smiles on their smooth round faces glanced casually at the disembarking passengers' credentials. I said that mine were being forwarded by air and they asked me politely to present them to the authorities when they arrived; they knew that I knew no one was going to expend energy on such formalities, and we exchanged cat-like smiles and I departed.

The tiny harbour was too small for large ships to dock, and I was rowed in a small boat from the ship to the dark wharf. There were no street lamps in the town, candles and lamps flickered and glimmered in the tiny shops, some of them no more than a recess in a coral wall, and the mysterious alleys were chequered with specks of light and pools of shadows. In the morning, I saw that the dilapidated buildings were faded pinks and greens, most of them had wooden shutters and balconies and the balconies trailed pots of ferns and leaves. Often the meanest hovel boasted a massive carved and studded Zanzibar door.

I would have fallen under the spell of the island without the balconies or the ferns or the carved doors, for I have a mania for narrow streets and in Zanzibar there is a perfect labyrinth of them. Some are so narrow two bicycles cannot pass – I know, I was riding one. As the island of Lamu, with streets so narrow in some places two people cannot pass, remains for me an island

CIRCLE VI

of colours and sounds, so I will always associate Zanzibar with a rich variety of colours and smells: great mounds of over-ripe fruit lying on the ground, Arabian stalls of curried potatoes and roasting kebab and strong black coffee. African stalls of roasting mealies and smoked octopus and hot cassava peppers. I tried everything, from oily Arabian candy to *chui*, the crown of a coconut tree and considered a great delicacy.

Outside the town there was the whiff of cloves and the sweet soporific scent of frangipani. The perfume, the lush green grass of the coconut groves, the lazy blue of the sky and the blue tranquillity of the water make me think of Tennyson's *The Lotos-Eaters*: 'All around the coast the languid air did swoon ... while warm air lulls us, blowing lowly ... We have had enough of action ... Surely, surely slumber is more sweet than toil ... we will not wander more.'

No description could capture the atmosphere of the island more perfectly. But I wonder, as I stand with the girls watching the dhows in the old port of Mombasa, for how long. The friends I stayed with in their house above the water say that even the Chinese and the East Germans have not been able to make any radical changes or deep impressions as yet; life still continues very much as before. The spritely little Arab with the gallant manners and lively brown eyes they took me to visit is still living in his bare stone bungalow amongst the profusion of bougainvillaea by the sea, he still brews coffee for them in a copper jug on the veranda, plies them with halva and sugary drinks, and barbecues chickens down on the shore. The little hotel hasn't changed either; it is still as sleepy and rickety as before.

We watch the Swahilis toting their loads and listen to their chanting; merchants curse and bargain; the water gleams still and bright as a sheet of metal and the dhows look like ancient cameos set in a blue stone.

When we leave the port and walk back through the alleys, the cars entangled in the narrow one way streets remind us that it is, after all, the twentieth century. The girls look for silver trinkets from Lamu and stones from Zanzibar, examine Chinese jade and African carvings and dishes from Tibet. At the African market they choose *kangas*; there is stall upon stall of them and still more deck the narrow Indian bazaar. Here in the bazaar china and glassware, Indian pots and vases and woven African mats and baskets overflow out of the shops and into the alley. Leaving the girls to rummage on their own I look for pottery. Not far off, on a street corner, an old woman in purdah is sitting on the ground surrounded by clay bowls; a few of the larger ones are genuine tribal pots. I select the ones I want and a younger woman, also in purdah, stands watching me.

'I think' she says in Swahili, 'that you like our Swahili pots very much.'

'Yes,' I reply. 'Truly I like them very much.'

'What will you use them for?' she laughs. 'Will you cook your food in them?'

'Of course,' I say seriously, 'I will cook maize flour and vegetables in them.'

She chuckles, then watches me thoughtfully for a while. Finally she asks; 'And what tribe is your husband?' It is, after all, the only possible deduction!

Dusk begins to fall and the little shops twinkle gaudily, white-robed Arabs sit cross-legged on the grass islands in the centre of the road playing cards; others brew coffee on the pavement in tall brass jugs and clink the tiny, handleless cups to

CIRCLE VI

attract customers. Women in saris glide past, sandals click softly, sailors sidle out of alleys like figures in an *apache* dance and the eyes of the children seem to glow larger and darker out of the dusk.

We drive home, past the palm trees and the baobabs, and the burnt out sun dying in the great hearth of the sea.

CIRCLE VII

The Nomads and the Stone Deserts of the North

SOMETHING happens when you cross the border into the north of Kenya. The land opens up, the distances brim over and engulf you and the rest of the world seems hardly to exist. But together with the physical change, a psychological metamorphosis takes place as well. Things swing into proportion, values shuffle themselves like a pack of cards and there is a new sense of harmony; with it, that special sense of freedom that seems to come with remoteness of the bush and vastness of the desert.

A small portion of the north of Kenya is sand desert, much of it is rock, volcanic hills and lava stones, the rest scrub and semi-scrub. Its inhabitants are nearly all nomads, Hamites for the most part and keepers of camels. I first came into contact with them some years ago on a safari to Lake Rudolf. It was my first taste of the desert too and so more than a safari, an experience. It was also the most gruelling and the most exciting journey I have been on.

I do not know to this day why I longed so fervently to go to Lake Rudolf. It was the embodiment of all the things for which, at the time, I still had no great love: the huge spaces, the parched earth. Perhaps since opposites must contain themselves I had all the time been attracted to the very things I had thought most vehemently to dislike. Certainly the mystery of the lake attracted me: its remoteness and inaccessibility, the strangeness of its scenery I had so often heard described, the fury of the gales and the turbulence of the sudden squalls. Few explorers had attempted to reach the hostile 'South Island' or 'Island of No Return' as it is often called, and of those who had, more than one had drowned.

There was no air strip at this time, no accommodation for tourists whatsoever, and few of the local population had managed to visit the lake – although everyone wanted to. The Government discouraged travellers to this part of the country too and even today one is obliged to travel in convoy.

There is no water and there are no sign posts in the regions that lie beyond the border dividing northern Kenya from the south. Further on, much further on, the earth road dwindles into a track which in turn disappears into the sand and the stones. It is easy to get lost or run out of water or petrol, and a check is kept on the few travellers who enter this territory. This is the reason for the 'border' between north and south; this too is the reason one must obtain a pass before crossing, and stop and sign the police book at the sentry post just beyond the little frontier 'town' of Isiolo.

We were an enormous convoy: an American power waggon, a Mercedes Unimog, two Land-Rovers and two lorries. The power waggon and the Unimog each had a winch; we were to need them. There was also an articulated trailer carrying a forty foot fishing boat: the object of the safari was to convey this boat across hundreds of miles of volcanic hills and lava stones to the lake. This was Monty's responsibility, for his firm had been given the dubious task of transporting the boat to its destination.

Early one morning we set off from Nairobi: two white hunters, two drivers, a photographer, the ship's captain and twenty-five African workers. There were supposed to be no women on so arduous a trip and like a stowaway, I joined the party a few miles out of town.

I think it was when the *askari* in his neat khaki uniform and Foreign Legion style hat lifted the barrier to let us pass across the border, then lowered it again behind us, that I had the strange sensation I had left the rest of the world behind me. And in a sense, I had. At first there was bush. Then gradually it began to thin out until there were only stones and massive outcrops of rocks and delicate acacia trees with spidery arms and silvery thorns. In the distance there were mountains, two and three tiers deep, and through gaps between them the plain flowed endlessly towards a non-existent horizon. It was hot and it was dusty and there was the constant glare of the sun. My throat was continually parched but I soon discovered it was useless to drink, five minutes later I was just as thirsty again and I must simply accept the state of dehydration and forget about it.

Sitting high up in that Unimog with Monty, the engine boiling away between us, the temperature averaged 110° F. But partly because I had been allowed to go on that safari as a special privilege, partly because I was the only woman, I made up my mind to give no one the chance to regret the favour or to condemn my sex. If the temperature rose to 130° F or we were down to the last glass of water I was determined not to let it throw me. With the result, of course, seeing that it is attitudes which are really of importance in life and not circumstances, nothing did.

There was a respite to the heat on the second day though, a

sort of Shangri-La it seemed to me. Suddenly we began climbing out of the hot stones and dry grass into a tumble of green hills, upward into rain forest and rocky slopes and thick tufty grass. I couldn't believe the transformation in the scenery and the air. When we reached the top, it was like standing on a platform; a green, breezy platform that lifts its head clear out of the thirsting wastelands into the cool rain and the clouds, while way below, stretching to the horizon in every direction, shimmered the parched grass and the burning stones.

Only a handful of civil servants and a padre were living on 'The Mountain' as Marsabit is often called. I remember the policeman particularly: he wore a little gold ring in one ear and told us of wild trips to the northern end of Lake Rudolf, and encounters with the fierce Gabra and Gelubba who still swoop down on the occasional tribal raid. He would chug along the water's edge in his little boat taking the odd pot shot at the trouble-makers, and sometimes get embroiled in a skirmish on land. He related his adventures with a lusty vivacity and his pirate's earring glinted in the lamplight; I couldn't take my eyes off it.

In the morning, while the men were checking their vehicles, I went for a walk in the hills, up towards the rain forest and Lake Paradise that Martin and Osa Johnson, the two American explorers, had discovered in their aquaplane in the 1930s. Fungus hung from the trees like frail green stalactites and there was a strong, fresh wind blowing. A jeep stopped beside me and a friendly voice called out: 'I shouldn't go any further if I were you, it's full of elephant up there!' It was the padre. He had, he said, been marooned in his house the whole of the previous day.

That afternoon, one of the white hunters took us out to look for Ahmed, the biggest tusker in East Africa and famous throughout the land. It was the first time I had tracked elephant on foot, and the thrill of the experience has never palled. We tried to find Lake Paradise too, but without success. Some years later, when at last Monty and I returned to Marsabit, we were to camp on its shores.

Before leaving the following morning, we filled all the petrol tanks to the brim at the solitary pump that stood amongst a handful of sleepy dukas. From Marsabit to the lake, we would have to rely on our own supplies. An African pumped the petrol laboriously by hand, a warrior leant against his spear, others lolled against a wall. Flies were left unmolested on their faces, the sun shone, no one spoke, no one moved. A woman in purdah examined a painted enamel bowl. She looked like a Boran, the tribe of fierce warrior riders who had galloped southwards from the Horn of Africa a hundred years ago. Although many of them have converted to the faith of Islam, they have still retained their old tribal customs. I had watched some of these people the day before at a well sunk cool and deep in the rocks at the foot of a range of hills; standing on ledges at various levels they passed buckets of water from one to the other. Now, in the distance, I could see a chain of camels filing towards the well, and our vehicles seemed crassly incongruous.

At the foot of the Mountain, heat waves and sunlit reaches waited to engulf us. Rocky mounds and protuberances seemed to stand out in all that space with an extra dimension, and the stoney earth began to unfold itself lap upon lap like a cardboard paper ocean. Despite the heat, there was always a light, warm breeze and not a particle of humidity; only in that Unimog was it like a furnace. Even so, I felt a strange excitement, a response to the wild freedom of this arid, uncompromising country and my first taste of the distances of the desert.

It was a relief each evening when the sun set, the glare softened and the breeze grew cooler. The temperature in these regions at night is perfect and we slept beneath the stars – the sky was packed tight with them, blanched almost white. I will never forget the way the first drink of the evening tasted when we stopped for the night – water had taken on a completely different connotation for me. To wash in so precious a commodity was the height of luxury, the cool feel of it on my skin and the removal of the day's caked sweat and dust was compensation enough for the hardest of days.

It always seemed to me at night that the whole world was wrapped up in a cocoon of darkness, our fire the only beacon, our little group the only living beings. The distances had enveloped us in their invisible embrace and marooned us like the waters of a flood. But this was by no means an unpleasant sensation and I frequently found myself completely preoccupied trying to absorb this feeling of heightened awareness which, in essence, is what it was. The suggestion of infinity made by the sky or the desert or the sea leads one's sights furthest away from oneself – and right back to the heart of the matter at the same time.

When the African safari crew lit the fire and prepared supper, it was the perfect time for Chui ('Leopard') Engelbrecht, the South African driver, to dip into his fund of tales. Has anything not happened to Engelbrecht that could possibly happen to man in Africa? Weather-beaten, wiry, his shorts and shirts always creased and crumpled, he would tell us how he shot waterfalls on a raft and ended up amongst the crocodiles, how he suffered from exposure, and thirst, tick fever and malaria, was wounded by game, bogged in the desert and lost. No bride south of the Sahara had been on a honeymoon such as Engelbrecht's. He dragged her in her high heels through bush and across sand until finally he had to put the poor girl in a blanket hoisted to two poles and carry her, with the help of his African tracker, like a dead antelope. Engelbrecht was afraid of nothing – except sand; when he spoke of it, his face broke out into a sweat. This was his fourth attempt to reach the lake: on every previous occasion he had been foiled by sand and it was on one of these safaris that he almost died of exposure.

The tall, easy-going white hunter with the ready smile and the Irish lilt talked of his sweet Ireland – what else? The ship's captain, rugged, complicated, hardened, told us of a fishing trip to Miami and goggling in the Caribbean. The other white hunter, quiet, good natured, spoke of the fishing camp that was being built near the lake by his firm of hunters. It was one of his clients who had sent the boat all the way from the United States to research the waters of the lake. From Monty I learned about the peculiarities of the game in the Northern Frontier (or North Eastern Province as it is now prosaically called); of the Grevy zebra that differs from the Burchell's further south in its close, narrow black stripes, its larger, more compact build, its fringed ears and thick mane. It is a far more handsome creature. The giraffe too are different in these regions. The Masai giraffe looks as though it has been daubed with white spots of paint, but in the north a network of white lines seems to have been drawn across its coat and, for this reason, it is called reticulated. As for the ostrich, we would see the Somali type with blue-grey necks and thighs, and there were gerenuk as well; these animals are especially suited to regions where there is little rainfall because they can go for long periods without drinking, obtaining the moisture they require from the grass and leaves on which they feed. Leaves in such regions are often very small and very tough so that they can resist heat and retain a certain amount of moisture.

Monty also mentioned tarantulas. They were my one fear on that safari: when we slept under a fever tree, I half expected to see one swinging down from a branch above me and every morning I would swivel a stick in my shoe before putting it on. . . .

During the days that followed we caught an occasional glimpse of game and, very rarely, of nomad youths leading a string of camels. But once we came upon a Rendille village.

The villagers appeared to be as unfamiliar with us as we were with them. The men wore goatskin sarongs, they were tall and slim and good looking with fine, proud faces. Hamites, like so many of Kenya's nomadic tribes, they had pushed their way down from Egypt and North Africa. Their faces were lean, inclined to narrowness, their noses straight, occasionally hooked, their mouths fine-cut. The women were slender and graceful with high cheek-bones and large eyes. Some wore only a goatskin skirt, others a sarong that passed over one shoulder and one breast. Like the Masai, wrist to elbow, ankle to calf, they were covered in metal bracelets, while many layers of necklaces made from palm fibres and polished with fat adorned their necks. Loops of the same fibre were threaded through their earlobes, and their heads and foreheads were adorned with beaded leather bands. The children wore nothing at all, save perhaps a belt made of threaded fragments of ostrich shell.

I was impressed immediately by a certain charm of manner, a courtesy and a dignity, a grace and a pride that both intrigued and attracted me. As soon as I returned home I went straight to the excellent Africana room of the Nairobi library to see what information I could find on these people. The windows of this room look out on to a Muslim mosque. It has silver domes and between them, in silver writing on a green wall is written: 'None to be worshipped but Allah. Muhammed is his prophet.' As I searched the shelves, browsing through wonderful old leather-bound books, forgotten and covered in dust, the muezzin's voice startled me, booming a command from his minaret. Several hours later, when the muezzin lustily summoned the devout to prayer yet again, I had been able to find out little more about the Rendille than I had already observed myself – their grace and their manners. Their origins were 'uncertain' and there was no information on their beliefs or their customs other than one extraordinary cult: it seems that these people have a strange practice of cutting into and deepening the navel depression. It is a rite peculiar to this tribe and perhaps, if the information is correct – I have not found it substantiated elsewhere – they perform this rite instead of circumcision. I had also read in a series of papers on Kenya's tribes that missionaries (all unsuccessful as the missionaries always are amongst the nomads) considered the Rendille a tribe of ascetics 'stinting themselves to the point of self-denial'. A few years later, the book called *The Samburu* by Paul Spencer was to appear and to my delight, I found a few pages on the Rendille.

It seems that in common with the Masai, an outbreak of smallpox depleted them at the end of the last century. The herds in turn suffered because there was a shortage of men to tend them. Totally reliant on their camels for sustenance, if their stocks do not increase, neither do the Rendille. It is a vicious circle of which Spencer seems to think they themselves are aware.

Like the Samburu with their cattle, the young men leave the village with part of the herds and find suitable pastures where they may remain for weeks at a time. They may be miles from a water point, but the young men will accept as a matter of course a walk of forty miles across their burning and usually shadeless country. Nor do they ride their camels. Spencer suggests this may be a lack of knowledge, or simply that the terrain is too rough. The young men are subject to stern discipline from their parents and guardians (when a tribalist is initiated he is given a sponsor, or a guardian, very much like the Western godfather in role); it is a part of that discipline with which they must equip themselves in order to grapple with the rigours of their life. Spencer writes that he believes it would be fair to say that 'Whereas a Samburu elder constantly worries about his youngest wife when she is out of sight, the Rendille worries about his camels'. But then there is a shortage of women amongst the polygamous Samburu, and a shortage of camels amongst the usually monogamous Rendille.

The Rendille are not easy-going people, and it is not simply the matter of the disciplines imposed upon them by their lives. They are much addicted to use of the curse, and family tensions arise as the result of the traditional inheritance by the eldest son of all his father's cattle. A younger son is also expected to assist and respect his elder brother; in return, when the younger son wishes to marry, he may expect fraternal – and also paternal – assistance in finding the eight camels he needs in order to pay the bride-price. Forced marriages would only be inflicted on a girl of any tribe by a bad father or extenuating circumstances; the custom is exactly the same as the Western system of dowry, but in reverse: it is the man who must find it instead of the woman.

The Rendille are traditional allies of the Samburu, amongst whom we camped at Maralal, but their territory begins where that of the Samburu ends, so that they have had less contact with Europeans. Some of them, like the Rendille we came across on our way to the lake, had certainly never been close to a white man.

I found myself standing apart with a pretty young woman. I didn't speak Rendille nor she Swahili, but she smiled and lifting a shy hand, touched first my skin and then my hair. She was intrigued by my clothes, the buttons especially, and curious to know whether beneath them my body was the same as hers. Her life was basic and so were her interests; the motor cars and the boat were completely out of context and aroused no interest in the villagers at all. She cradled her arms and pretended to rock a baby and looked at me with an enquiring smile. I nodded my head and she frowned and opened slender hands, palm upwards, in an eloquent gesture of interrogation and surprise, where then were my children? She touched my back: why was I not carrying them with me? It was inconceivable to her that a woman should be separated from her child – a baby especially. I felt guilty and stretching my arm out shoulder height, indicated with a wordless lie that they were already half grown. She asked me where I came from then, pointing first to me and then in the general direction of the horizon. I pointed far into the distance and pushed my lips forward, African fashion, to signify that I had come from afar. She nodded and beckoned me to squat beside her in front of her hut. A woman passed, bearing a gourd of water from the green and fetid well; the sun beat down on the stoney earth, vultures clustered voraciously round the remains of a dead camel not far from the village. I asked her permission to look into the hut and she smilingly aquiesced. It was pointed and built of a light, collapsible framework of sticks over which had been thrown goatskins and a layer of palm thatch to keep the interior cool. It was light and odourless inside (unlike the interior of Masai dwellings) and on the ground a reed mat and the charred remains of a fire between two stools. A couple of vessels resembling calabashes hung from the wooden framework. There was nothing else, apart from a cooking pot and an enamel bowl which she must have purchased at Marsabit. The dead camel suggested she may have cooked one of her rare meals of meat the previous evening. The Rendille do not kill for meat and eat it only when one of their herds dies a natural death; like the Masai, they subsist on a diet of milk mixed with blood painlessly drawn from the animal's jugular vein.

The harsh simplicity of the land demanded a harsh simplicity of living and she possessed only what was essential. And if the sun-steeped plains that offered neither shade nor water nor grass had imposed upon her people the most rigorous discipline, it had also afforded them, in exchange, certain privileges. Their bodies unhampered by clothes or possessions, their minds as uncluttered as the distances that had conceived them, they wandered free as the desert breeze, dependent only upon their camels – and upon themselves.

The glare began to soften, the sun trailed dusty cobwebs across the earth and the harsh line of the hills softened and blurred. That night we slept beneath a tall thorn tree. Stars seemed caught in the branches like silver fishes in a net, and above the tree the moon shone still and pale as a pond of clear water.

The following day we skirted the Chalbi Desert – we were to have reason to remember it on our homeward journey – and stopped at the God-forsaken police post of North Horr.

A group of thatched huts was neatly arranged round an empty circle of sand, in its midst a tall mast from which fluttered a lone Union Jack. Mocked by the empty desert, last remnant of homage to a declining power, the askaris all had to salute the flag when they came in. The plump, expansive little English policeman in charge told us that the Goan officer under him subjected them to a stroke of the cane if they omitted the ritual; it all sounded pathetically Kiplingesque.

In his tiny, sweltering office, the policeman radioed Marsabit to inform them of our safe arrival. He also provided us with a guide who, he hoped, would be able to direct us to the lake – the guides themselves sometimes get lost in that area, he added casually. He also mentioned with equal nonchalance that two people had thirsted to death a couple of years ago in the area. But he made it all sound very cheerful.

Perhaps it was the policeman's words, or perhaps it was because there was no police post at the lake to radio Marsabit or even North Horr should we fail to arrive, that the terrain seemed to me yet wilder and more desolate than before. A faint wheel track left in the sand beneath the stones by the last vehicle that had passed that way many weeks previously, and the dubious directions of our guide, were all we had to go by. A compass in these regions is of no avail – the iron content in the rock throws its calculations.

I took turns in travelling in the various vehicles. One day, with Monty in the Unimog, a fantastic apparition appeared in the midst of all that nothingness: a white man, wearing shorts and shirt and a pair of thonged sandals like the nomads. He

The author watching the millions of flamingoes at Lake Nakuru

Monty and Mandy share a joke on safari

Mandy's first meeting with the Samburu girls

Smiles and laughter made their own language

As man moves in, the elephants are forced out

Leopard at Serengeti

The trailer carrying the boat across the stone deserts of the north

CIRCLE VII

walked like a nomad too, with the same long, springy gait. He smiled, waved, enquired whether everything was all right, and before we had time to catch our breaths and ask whence he came and whither he was going, passed on. Mad dogs and Englishmen, I muttered to Monty. . . . Months afterwards, we were to discover that this man was an anthropologist living mostly with the Samburu, and partly with the Rendille. It was in fact Paul Spencer, whose book on these people was to appear two or three years later.

Another day I was travelling with the tall, spare, very polite, very English photographer. He always managed to look neat, washed and uncrumpled with a sort of evenness of tone and appearance I delightedly watched thrown out of gear that afternoon.

We caught sight of literally hundreds of camels filing along the top of a rocky line of hills. A caravan of camels is always fascinating; but the curves of their bodies and the curves of the hills outlined against that clear sky was quite spectacular. The photographer veered away from the convoy and charged up into the range of hills. We stopped within a hundred yards of the mass of camels. Then he leapt out of the Land-Rover, grabbed his tripod, thrust a heavy bag into my hand and raced off, shouting to me to follow. Adjusting his tripod, he snapped commands at me in the manner of a surgeon in a Hollywood film. Unfortunately camera equipment in those days was still a mass of esoteric gadgets as far as I was concerned. Fumbling nervously with unidentifiable objects that I knew were worth hundreds of pounds, I watched the camels and the herdsmen advancing towards us. Suddenly, the youths and the warriors broke into a run and charged forward, brandishing their spears.

'Quick,' the photographer shouted, incoherently, 'jump into the car. I can't possibly tip all of them. I'll throw them something as we drive off. Help me with this stuff. Come on. *Hurry!*'

Reversing his instructions, I helped him with the equipment then got into the car – just as the first warrior bore down on us. The wheels skidded, the vehicle moved off and the photographer chucked two or three fifty-cent pieces out of the window. The warriors came pelting after us.

I am sure the tribesmen didn't want any money – at this time they still bartered for goods in these regions. Quite possibly they didn't even know what the strange looking apparatus the cameraman was pointing at them was either; they simply objected to having it pointed at them. We would have done better to photograph the picturesque scene from the foot of the hills. As it was, we had to catch up with the rest of the convoy and so didn't get any photographs at all.

It took us six days to reach the lake. In the last two we covered sixty-five miles. There were sand luggas (sand rivers) and there were rocks impeding our way. The largest sand river we had to cross stretched for four hundred yards. It was called the K.A.R. lugga because vehicles of the King's African Rifles had stuck there in World War II.

We stuck there too. It was then that I began to understand about sand.

First, the lorries had to be towed across. A single winch was insufficient and so the power-waggon had to be winched to the Unimog, the lorry to the power-waggon. I watched from the side of the lugga, where a few stunted bushes had taken root. All round me the sun-dazed land rolled in stoney laps towards the hazy horizon, and the quiet and the heat seemed to throb.

CIRCLE VII

Suddenly engines began to scream and strain; winches were stretched taut and the sweat began pouring off the men's backs and faces. Slowly the lorry moved forward across the lugga.

The real problem was that long, heavy trailer carrying the boat. Even two winches were insufficient. When the winches were strained to their utmost and it seemed to me that the engines must burst, still that trailer would not budge. The men began hacking branches from the bushes then and these they placed in front of the trailer like a runway. Using both winches once more, they managed to pull the vehicle across the fifteen yards of sand covered by the branches. Then they picked up the improvised runway and laid it down in front of the vehicle once more. I found myself working out fifteen into four hundred yards. Before I could finish the calculation, one of the winches broke. It flew wildly to one side, just missing one of the men and narrowly avoiding a nasty accident.

The men clustered round the power-waggon examining the extent of the damage and assessing the possibility of repair. It was a tense few moments because without the winch we would be unable to get the boat across the lugga. But a repair job was possible and the trailer continued its painfully arduous crossing.

It took an entire day. It was sunset by the time we were all finally the other side of that lugga. I think I was the last to cross, all the vehicles were already safely beached when a Land-Rover returned to fetch me. I remember how the wheels began skimming round when they lost their grip on the sand, and wondering if we would make it to the other side.

We camped where we emerged from the lugga. There was not a tree, not an outcrop of rock. Just the stones and the darkening sky, and in the distance a stark range of hills. I remember how bizarre the table looked that night, a tiny, incongruous symbol of another world lost in an abyss of space, rather like a Surrealist painting.

We were always caked in dust and sweat at the end of a day, and strained from the long hours of glaring sun; but that evening exhaustion and exposure seemed to add subtle shades to the creases and hollows in the men's faces, some of whom now had a five day growth of beard. I found myself thinking of the early East African explorers of the last century; compared to the hardships and deprivations they had suffered, this safari was easy. They had covered hundreds of miles on foot, sometimes stricken with fever or mad with thirst. Food supplies dwindled, cattle and pack donkeys – and often porters – died. Tribes were hostile. Sometimes, when it rained, they had no shelter from the tropical downpour other than the flanks of an animal. Yet still they continued, reached their destination, achieved their object, returned home to England or Europe – and came back again. Perhaps it is because the world is losing its challenge that students feel the need to riot. There has to be something to replace suffragettes and heretics, Dada-ists – and explorers.

The breeze always blew light and cool of an evening, but that night one felt an especial gratitude for the divine favour – and water was like an elixir granted to their favourites by the gods. I think with each day that passed we took it less and less for granted; but after days of space and sun and sky much that was formerly important seems trivial; one's perspective appears to broaden as the distances widen.

The following day there were more luggas. There were also rocks that had to be moved out of the way and large dips that had to be filled in with stone and sand before we could cross.

CIRCLE VII

Sometimes a driver would try and charge a lugga, but he never succeeded. As soon as he felt himself beginning to stick he would rev the engine, the wheels would begin to spin then start to disappear into the sand. Were he to continue, it wouldn't take very long to bury the entire vehicle. No wonder Engelbrecht was afraid of sand.

On the sixth day we came to a grim barrier of hills. I felt, as we drove deeper and deeper into them, that we would never get out. The hostile slopes were scattered with black lava stones and grey-green sand. There was not a blade of grass, not a shadow of shade. With each fresh ascent, we saw another empty valley below us and another barren summit ahead, the sky resting upon it light as an unfurled bolt of blue voile. The starkness of the hills had a mythological quality about them, they were endless; our fate decreed by the gods to wander up and down them eternally.... Quite suddenly, we emerged from the range and found ourselves on top of a precipitous escarpment. At its foot, lay the lake.

It was a shattering sight after all those burnt and waterless miles. I began to understand what Teleki and his men must have felt when they discovered the lake less than a hundred years ago. It stretched to the horizon like the sea and its colour that day was cool, translucent green. The volcanic hills curved away on either side of us and disappeared into the distance with the shore line. A few miles further out we could see the Isle of No Return, its sharp, sandy pink slopes so bare they looked as though they had been shaved. Rocks broke like waves at the foot of the escarpment, and the incline separating them from the lake itself was covered with the same grey-green sand and black lava stones as the hills. A few stunted thorn trees were scattered across it, and half way between the foot of the escarpment and the water was a cluster of doum palms. Only by the water's edge was there grass, a thin, lime-green band. It was desolate and harsh and still, but the stillness was fraught with the cries of a thousand birds and the land, throbbing with heat, seemed to wait with bated breath. . . .

The water of the lake is brackish, but cutting through the doum palms like the silver blade of a knife, we found a trickle of spring water. I knelt and cupped my hands and drank, and found that it was fresh and sweet. Neither pharaoh nor sultan nor emperor has received a gift more precious than a spring of sweet water in a land as arid and parched as that.

As though to compensate for the barrenness of the earth a marvellous variety of birds frequent the shores: flamingo and ibis, pelicans and fish eagles, cormorants and sand-pipers, kingfishers, wild geese, herons, plovers and many more.

When the sun set that evening, it seemed to melt and spread across the water like golden wax. Later the stars appeared, thorn trees hung like cobwebs in the windy spaces of the night and the moon shone down on a pearl and pewter earth.

The village of El Molo was only a few miles from our camp amongst the palms, and Monty and I went to visit it one afternoon. Von Höhnel, in his book *Discovery by Count Teleki of Lakes Rudolf and Stefanie*, says that El Molo means 'Poor Devil'. Certainly the village must be the most desolate in all the world. A group of straw huts like inverted bird's nests and not much more commodious stand naked to the sun on flat lava rocks by the edge of the lake. When we drove up, fishermen were standing in a circle holding a net in the water; sometimes they use harpoons made from the roots of acacia trees. They hunt crocodile with these harpoons – and hippos too, although we never saw any near that area of the lake. The men wait until the hippo begins to make for the shore, then they submerge themselves in the water. One member of the party remains by the edge of the lake, and it is up to him to shout and gesticulate in order to frighten the animal who will then return to the safety of the water. Immediately, the men attack with their harpoons. Then they truss him up with ropes (made, I imagine, from palm fibres) and drag him back to the shore. His flesh provides a little variety to their monotonous diet of tilapia and Nile perch caught in the lake, and the tough husk of the doum palm nut which they pound to a powder. As though the lives of the villagers are not austere enough, the water of their lake is not even sweet.

How terrible the discovery of the water's brackishness had been when Count Teleki and his men ran down to the water to drink! Von Höhnel writes: 'Although utterly exhausted, after seven hours march in the intense and parching heat, we felt our spirits rise once more as we stood upon the beach at last, and saw the beautiful water, clear as crystal, stretching away before us. The men rushed down shouting, to plunge into the lake, but soon returned in bitter disappointment; the water was brackish!'

Faced with hunger and thirst, Teleki and his men managed to drink the water just as the El Molo do. But it does not improve the health of the villagers already impaired by an inadequate diet and years of intermarriage. Children appeared from the village as we stood watching the fishermen. They were thin and some had rickets, a very different build from the lithe suppleness of the nomads.

An old man hobbled up to us, greeted us and enquired whether we would like some fish. We accepted out of courtesy and the old man yelled lustily to the fishermen. I asked him where he had learned to speak Swahili. He smiled his toothless smile, well pleased with his accomplishment, and explained with his skeleton vocabulary that once a white man had come to the village. But he was unable to explain who he was or how long he had stayed; perhaps he was a missionary.

'Where,' I asked him, 'are the women?'

He pointed to the huts. 'They sleep,' he said. 'They sleep all day.'

I laughed. 'Do they not cook your fish?'

'Sometimes. Sometimes we eat it raw.'

'What else do you eat?'

'Nothing else.'

There were some goats in the distance, a hardy breed able to subsist on the meagre vegetation by the lake.

'Are those yours?'

'They are ours.'

'And do you not drink their milk?'

'When there is no rain there is no milk.'

Rain, I thought wryly, looking at that barren land where rain hardly ever fell. But I knew that the Government had offered to settle the El Molo in a more hospitable area, and they had said: 'There are more fish in the water than cows in the grass', and refused to go.

Two naked fishermen emerged from the water, each with a large tilapia in his hand. The old man took the fish and carried them to the Land-Rover, the children followed. We gave the old man beads in payment; one of the children grabbed a few out of his hand and ran off laughing. The others followed him. A raft slipped by, made of doum palms.

The El Molo say that many years ago some of their people sailed away on these rafts to the Isle of No Return. Slave

CIRCLE VII

traders had come to their village, and in order to escape them, some of the villagers fled to the island. They took as many goats and pots as possible – and strange to say, nothing is to be found on the island today other than snakes and scorpions, a few goats and a few broken pieces of pottery. None of the refugees ever returned and no one has any other explanation to offer for the mysterious presence of the goats on that God-forsaken isle.

It was commonly believed that the El Molo are dying out. But if there were a hundred of them twenty to thirty years ago, there are two hundred today. Either the previous count was inaccurate – or else the El Molo, like everyone else, are in fact now on the increase. As for their origins, no one is quite certain, and there are those who say they may be descended from the earliest people in Kenya.

For the next few days the men were busy building the jetty from which they would launch the boat. I watched them with one eye and with the other kept a look out for the sly crocodiles. Sometimes I would take a walk along the shore, sometimes I remained in camp, wrote a little or read. It was hot in the morning, that was the time the wind dropped. At night, it howled dementedly amongst the palm fronds, chafing them together like rusty swords. Some of the palms were headless, others bent or sloping in crazy angles from years of buffeting by the infamous gales.

I was never alone in camp, there was always a handful of Rendille to keep me company. One of them used to bring his goat along, trailing it on a lead of plaited palm fronds. When one day one of our party offered him money for it, he examined the note carefully, shook his head uncomprehendingly and politely gave it back. He had never seen money before, and it delighted me to think that all the stockbrokers in London and all the financiers in Wall Street together could not buy his goat.

Sometimes a few Turkana dropped by, tall thin men carrying wooden head-rests so that when they slept they would not disarrange their elaborate coiffure. The young men wear a sort of chignon which they achieve by repeatedly fluffing out their hair with a stick, they then insert a hooped bar in the centre and dramatize the whole effect with a flourish of ostrich feathers. The women – whose bride-price in this tribe is unusually high and whose status is almost equivalent to the men's – twist their hair into thin strands that hang down rather like the fringes of a shawl.

The Turkana did not seem to me to have the same pride and graceful manners as the Rendille. Von Höhnel remarks in his book that they were the noisiest and wildest tribe he came across, while the Rendille look down upon them as children because they are so ill-disciplined. Perhaps it is because they do not practise circumcision and the responsibilities and seriousness of manhood are therefore not impressed upon them.

Both Turkana and Rendille watched the building of the jetty with indifference and I found myself wondering what they *did* think. When they stood so still and motionless for such long periods at a time, were their minds one with the earth and the sky, their heart-beats one with the pulse of the universe? How did it affect a man, all that space, and that different rhythm of living?

Finally the jetty was complete. A tall El Molo lady was persuaded to break a bottle of champagne against the side of the boat. Giggling and overcome with confusion, she complied.

It was then a terrible and totally unforeseen event occurred.

CIRCLE VII

The boat refused to leave the cradle. Down into the water the beautiful forty-footer headed, down went the stern, dunked by the cradle. The water began rushing in.

We had conveyed the boat hundreds of miles across some of the worst terrain in the world – only to have it sink the moment it touched water.

The men were running round in small circles shouting at one another. The photographer was of course shooting the scene with an almost demented intensity: Hollywood had to *stage* this sort of thing! The boat continued to sink, the men to yell at one another distractedly and run frantically to and fro, with utter futility; except for Monty, whom I suddenly noticed struggling with a stout piece of wood that had been used in the construction of the jetty. He was shouting at the African workmen to give him a hand and they helped him drag it to the jetty. He then jumped into the Unimog and rammed the pole against the side of the keeling craft, finally managing to shove her free of the cradle so that she righted herself in the water.

Monty and I never sailed in that boat. For some petty reason or grudge of his own which he shared with the ship's captain, the quiet, usually good-natured white hunter in charge of the expedition could not bring himself to invite Monty aboard. We were intrigued by these facets of the men's behaviour: you get to know people very well on safari.

The ship was afloat, our mission complete, and it was time to go. I didn't want to. The idea of nylon stockings and cocktail chat was quite abhorrent. Besides, I longed to explore the strange, hostile Isle of No Return with its barren slopes and rocks, its pottery and its goats. It was still worse for Monty; he had to go back to the confines of an office.

The Irish white hunter and Chui Engelbrecht came with us. We called by at the little police post at North Horr, and the policeman told us it was safe to take a short cut across the Chalbi Desert; we could follow the tracks he had made on his way to the police post some few weeks earlier.

I had not been in a sand desert before and I will never forget the Chalbi. The monotone terracotta colouring, the uniformly flat terrain that stretched away to the horizon in all directions began to give me a feeling of unease. Most of the time I found my eyes focused on those faint wheel tracks which were our only guide: what if they should suddenly disappear? When we stopped for a drink and I got out of the vehicle, I discovered that the firm surface of the sand was only a few, fragile inches deep. Beneath it, the soft, bottomless land seemed to crumble away into a subterranean eternity. There was not a single living thing, not an insect, not a bird. Nothing but the hot sun, the sky and the sand.

We travelled on, and now I began to feel trapped in space: the old feeling of agoraphobia that I had sometimes experienced when first I came to this country, the desire to ascend straight upwards towards the sky – it seemed the only way out. And then it happened. The tracks gave out. A great caravan of camels had passed that way, obliterating them entirely.

Leaving Engelbrecht sitting in his lorry to mark our point of departure, we began travelling in ever widening circles in the Land-Rover to see if we could pick up the tracks. Perhaps a light wind had blown sand over them, but we never found them again.

We drove on, passing the skeleton of a vehicle three-quarters sunk into the sand. The sight was eerie and not exactly reassuring. Then up came the gallant Engelbrecht: had he ever

CIRCLE VII

been known to lose his sense of direction? Off he careered in his ancient lorry, bravely taking the lead, only to find himself caught once again by his ancient enemy – sand.

We were too tired and too strained to dig the lorry out that night. For some time we had been driving in the brilliant moonlight, and we had started out at dawn. This time we did not dare use any of our scant water supply to wash away the dust and the sweat.

The men argued about the direction in which we were travelling, but finally reached a certain and unanimous agreement. In the morning however, according to their calculations, the sun rose in the West. We knew then we were indisputably lost.

I didn't doubt that we would find our way out of the desert, but the time and the space that separated us from that exit seemed to me infinite. I felt a strange sort of impatience. I didn't want to wait to eat breakfast. I thought the men would never finish digging Engelbrecht's lorry out of the sand. When we continued our journey, it seemed to me we were travelling at a snail's pace. I had no idea how much water and gas remained, and ostrich-like I preferred not to enquire.

That afternoon we came across a herd of camels – the first sign of life so far. They were standing by a green and fetid well that nourished a few weary thorn bushes. Next to the well sat three nomads. They were kneading sand with water from the well and with this mixture they were building a low curved wall which on its completion would serve as a trough for the camels.

We tried greeting them in Swahili. The oldest of the men, a wizened skeleton of a being, merely grunted and shook his head. He was dressed in a skin tunic, like his companions, and wore no ornaments. We thought they were Gabra or Gelubba – the aggressive tribesmen of which the policeman at Marsabit had spoken. A warrior appeared from nowhere and stood leaning on his spear which made a symmetrical angle with the slim, vertical line of his body. His hair was divided into numerous little plaits and well covered with mud and fat. He stood quite motionless and his expression was one of sullen pride and scorn. Slowly Monty repeated the word 'Marsabit' and waited enquiringly. We knew they were well acquainted with the name, for Marsabit is the administration centre for all that area, but they continued to stare at us blankly. We offered them some tobacco. They barely glanced at it, and continued kneading their sandy dough. The gaze of the warrior was unflickering and hostile.

'Let's get the hell out,' Monty said. And we left.

On we drove across that waveless brown ocean. It was only broken by mirages – water, hills, trees. We didn't even see the hoof marks of a camel. What, I wonder, would have happened to us had all the tribesmen proved as immune to bribery as the three characters by the well? But the next day we came across a lone figure who succumbed to the temptation of our gifts. At first he seemed equally hostile, but when he saw the tobacco, hesitated. Seizing on this faint indication of capitulation, Monty proffered more. The man weakened and nodded his head. This time, in response to the clearly reiterated syllables of Marsabit, he raised his arm and pointed into the distance.

We signalled to him to climb into the car but he shook his head disdainfully and walked ahead. For hours we crawled behind our arrogant guide; not once did he turn his head or give the slightest indication he was aware of our presence, until finally he stopped, turned, and waved his hand at a range of

CIRCLE VII

hills. Then he walked wordlessly past us, back in the direction whence he had come.

We drove on towards the hills, expecting them to dissolve, as they had done so often, into a shimmering expanse of water which in turn dissolved into sand. But they were solid stone, and they waited.

Return to Marsabit

I LONGED to return to the north of Kenya, drawn by its arid distances and fascinated by its nomadic people. Most of all, I wanted to go back to Marsabit, but the best part of a decade was to pass before I realized that desire. During this time, we did manage to revisit Lake Rudolf on one occasion, staying at a different part and following a different route that took us high into cool, green hills where we crossed the Equator at nine thousand feet, and down steep escarpments from whose summits we could see the limitless land slowly unfurling itself until it merged with a soft haze of sky.

We managed to sojourn amongst the nomads too, pitching our tents at Maralal amongst the Samburu. The site overlooked a dam and a glade of tall fever trees, there was a gentle escarpment behind us and a semi-circle of hills opposite. Dawn would find zebra drinking by the dam, impala licking salt from the mud and marabou storks perched like cantankerous old judges in the trees.

We encountered a rhino before we met the Samburu, we watched him making his myopic way towards our tents the morning of our arrival; perhaps we had camped in the middle of his daily route. The wind must have been blowing our scent away from him, for he continued walking towards us. When he was about fifteen yards off we made a wild dash for the safari car; the front doors were open but the canvas side flaps were battened down and Mandy made a spectacular dive straight through the narrow hatch above the front seat into the back: it is amazing what gymnastic feats one is capable of when threatened by an animal in the bush.

The rhino took over the camp, standing motionlessly (doubtless a little perplexed by the sudden commotion) next to one of the tents. A tick bird sat on his back, devouring the ticks that infested his skin; then suddenly the bird flew off with its urgent call signifying danger, and the rhino ambled away.

Afterwards the girls and I drove off to the little 'township' of Maralal. Beneath the blue sky and strong yellow sun, a mosaic of red and yellow cloaks swirled softly in the breeze, spears glinted, teeth glistened, dark eyes flashed; there were the slim, straight lines of the warriors, the flowing folds of the women's cloaks and the wide curves of a calabash.

We walked in the bright sunlight along the broad, dusty street flanked by mud dukas with tin roofs and divided by a strip of grass and a row of trees. The colourful crowd of people sauntered casually past. The women looked at the girls and me, at our faces and our hair and our clothes. They were pretty, with high cheek-bones and large eyes and a shy coquettishness, and they had taken great pains over the pretty designs marked lightly on their foreheads and their cheek-bones which seemed to indicate that their reputation for vanity was not without foundation. They walked gracefully, and I wondered what they thought of the clothes and the mascara and the lipstick of the West.

The warriors barely glanced at us. Conscious of their good looks, rivalling one another for the girls – whom they may not marry until they reach their late thirties and their long term of warriorhood comes to an end – there is an arrogance in their walk, and in their glance too when they deign to give it. It is in essence the same pride and independence of the Masai, birthright of all nomadic peoples, but in the harsher regions of the north it is accentuated because their lives are more austere.

As we drove away from the little 'town' cries of 'Stop, *stop!*' from the roof where the girls were perched brought me to a sudden halt.

Three small children came running towards us and on the grass I now saw the cause of all the excitement – a newly born goat, small, wet, woolly, trying to struggle to its feet.

The Samburu children were delighted with the appearance of Lissa and Mandy, and the delight was mutual. The youngest of them, a little boy with a plump face and an enormous smile that welled over his features and creased his merry little eyes, had a quality of such lovableness about him that Lissa, within moments, had him upon her lap. The two girls and the small boy could not speak Swahili and neither Lissa nor Mandy knew any Samburu, but smiles and laughter made their own language; there was a poignant significance in the scene and although the girls were not aware of it they have retained as nostalgic a memory of the encounter as I have myself.

Back at camp, Monty, who had been doing some photography, was trying to pacify three elderly ladies; convinced he had taken their picture, no reassurance would satisfy them or allay their fears. Finally, to distract them, he handed one of them his binoculars, focusing it on a donkey. She thought it was a camera and shrieked with delight when the animal zoomed into her amazed view. Enchanted by the powers of those magic eyes, she handed them to her companions, and the

CIRCLE VII

three old girls eventually departed talking and laughing, their suspicious indignation quite forgotten.

At night a bright white moon with a hard silver rim gilded the fever trees and flaunted itself above the hills. It grew cold then and we felt the drop in temperature keenly; even with a sweater on beneath a couple of blankets I was not immune to it. But morning brought the warmth of the sun, and hot coffee and mounds of toast. Samburu women in goatskin skirts with beaded trains would pass by the tents at this hour and climb the gently sloping escarpment: donkeys with wicker baskets followed behind. When they disappeared out of sight, we could hear the thud of pangas and their high calls for a while; then all was silent.

One morning Lissa and I followed in their footsteps; we wanted to explore the regions that lay behind the escarpment. It was quiet up there in the bushes and the warm red earth was scattered with boulders and stones. Occasionally a bird darted from a branch, or from the distance came the mournful cry of a red-beaked ground-hornbill, more like that of a goat than a bird. The behaviour of these birds during the breeding season is unique. The female collects pieces of mud in her beak with which she plasters the hole in the bark of a tree; when it is barely more than an inch or two wide, she finally squeezes herself inside. Thus incarcerated, safe from snakes and other predators, she lays her eggs. The male feeds her through the tiny hole she has left unsealed; should he die, she would starve to death. When the young birds are old enough to receive food from their father, the mother begins to hack away at the mud plaster with her beak until at last she is free. The chicks then seal it again with the sticky berries and slugs brought to them by the male. And there they stay until by some miraculous time-clock of nature they know that the time has come for them to chip away at the mud plastering and make their début (within twelve or twenty-four hours or more of each other, depending on when they were hatched) into the space and sunlight that lies beyond the confines of their tiny, dark little world.

Besides the cry of a hornbill, we suddenly heard the high calls of the Samburu women. We walked on, ranges of hills rising and falling like russet coloured waves in an ocean swell on either side of the plateau all the way to the horizon, until we came across the women in a clearing. Their donkeys were cruelly tethered to a bush by means of a wire passing through the animal's nostrils.

The women smiled and came over to us with their lithe, supple walk. Thin strips of leather sewn with beads and prettily patterned were threaded through the stretched lobes of their ears; rows of coloured beads adorned their necks. They knew a little Swahili and stayed to talk to us for a while, then they returned to their work, cutting fire-wood with their pangas.

Lissa and I left – Lissa turned in one direction, I in the opposite. Once again I had completely lost my bearings. Had Lissa not been with me, I wonder if I would ever have realized the fact: the view of those russet coloured hills stretching away on either side looked identical.

In the vicinity where we were camped, many of the slopes were grassy (these drier, russet tones were only visible further away) and there were fine herds of oryx nearby; when we drove slowly across the undulating grassland past scattered trees and bushes, horns would appear as though interwoven into a rich old tapestry of finely embroidered leaves and thorns. Fleet and powerful eland, mighty dewlaps swinging, would

CIRCLE VII

race along a hill top like a scene from some ancient frieze. They are the biggest of the antelope family and weigh between one and a half and two thousand pounds. But they are gentle creatures despite their bulk, and nimble as well; a heavy bull can clear an eight foot fence.

One afternoon, when Monty and the girls were down at the dam photographing the impala, I received a visit from two Samburu elders. Their heads were shaved and a blanket carelessly thrown round their bodies. Again, there was no common language but we greeted one another with nods and handshakes. One of them spat. I knew that spitting is considered a form of blessing amongst the Masai and that they and the Samburu, who are a related tribe, have much in common. But the manner in which this man expelled his spittle upon the red earth struck me as containing a larger element of disgust than blessedness. I might have been right, because glancing through A. C. Hollis's book *The Masai* sometime later I came across the following passage: 'The Masai have two ways of spitting, one is to show contempt, and the other astonishment. Besides this the medicine men spit when they wish to heal people. If a Masai wishes to show his contempt for another man, he expectorates a small stream of saliva forcibly through the hole in his teeth into the man's face and says at the same time: "You are a dog." Formerly when the Masai saw Swahilis they used to spit on the ground and say: "These coast people stink like fowls." '

What a pity Hollis omitted to include the Masai's expression when they sniffed the (to them) nauseating smell of the European!

My visitors stayed anyway. We looked at one another, nodded, smiled, exchanged a few leisurely ees and ahs and mms of varying lengths and tone. I had learnt to do this when I used to ride across the Kikuyu land which begins just beyond our garden. The old women would call out greetings to me (or shriek with helpless laughter if I chose to trot, a ridiculous spectacle to them) and engage me in long Kikuyu conversations of which I understood not a word. What I didn't realize in those early days was that the 'ee' I heard them frequently using, and which I reiterated in any long pause, was Kikuyu for yes, and I was simply agreeing with everything they said.

The two men squatted by one of the tents, quite at home, not particularly curious, but disinclined to move on. It was hot, and I was sleepy, and I went off to rest. When I awoke, the two men had gone, Monty had returned, and Lissa and Mandy were sitting with two young Samburu girls and a couple of toddlers.

One of the girls was enchanting, the expression on her heart-shaped face was sweet and shy, her movements graceful and her voice soft and gentle. We offered her tea. Immediately she gave the cup to the two little ones who between them drained it. We poured a second cup for her and again she gave it to the babies. We replenished it a third time and she handed it to her companion. Only when everyone else was satisfied did she sip of the liquid herself. Nor, when we gave her biscuits and dates, would she touch a morsel until the others had eaten their fill. When they left, we gave them a present of sugar and dates, which they consider luxuries.

Paul Spencer, in his book *The Samburu*, comments on the 'warmth and charm in their community living.' He emphasizes too the importance of the word 'respect' amongst these people, which includes respect for their ethics and their traditions. Often, the respect is enforced by self-discipline: a young *moran* might be tempted to eat the larger portion of his meat and give the smaller piece to a hungry elder. But an older moran, no matter how hungry, would always give away the larger portion just as this girl would always put the needs of her companions before her own. Without this self-discipline and unselfish hospitality, similar to the Arab nomads of the desert, these people would be unable to survive the harshness of their lives. Lissa asked one of the girls (who spoke Swahili) her age, but she didn't know. Tribesmen in this country belong to age groups whose members are as closely knit as brothers and sisters. All of them are initiated into each new phase of their lives at the same time, so that they take into account not the number of years that have passed but the particular stage to which they have progressed – girlhood, womanhood, wife. Again there is that different stress on the meaning (or meaninglessness) of time. Spencer writes of his sojourn amongst the Samburu: 'While Africa to the south of us was in the throes of an industrial revolution struggling towards a golden age of the future, we were living – foolishly perhaps – in the golden age of the present. Time meant something quite different; and under this spell, three years of my life slipped past unnoticed.'

The Samburu girls took their leave of us. I watched them depart in single file, each of them finely made as though in this hard life of theirs nothing is in excess or abundance and the balance of their lives – that balance between starvation and sufficiency – is so delicately held even their bodies are not permitted an ounce of surplus flesh.

They climbed the hill the other side of the water, a fragile thread weaving earth to sky in that same harmony of form which is the intrinsic quality of any real art – or the best moments of life itself.

Dusk fell, and from the heart of the gathering darkness echoed that high, whirring hum which is the pulse of the African night. The Samburu girls had left a strong impression on us and Lissa and Mandy discussed the advantages and disadvantages of tribal life. They were very much in favour of age groups instead of birthdays, having noticed the European preoccupation with time. Mandy, who resented the rote learning of school and was convinced she would learn far more from all the books she wanted to read, was equally persuaded that she gained far more from three days in the bush than three months at school. She therefore considered the fact that these girls didn't go to school was a greater advantage than loss. But what about all the art and literature in the world? Lissa, who had agreed with her most of the way, demurred. Mandy shrugged and the conversation was left in mid-air. It was obvious to both of them that there are advantages on both sides. It is a point I have often argued with guests at the dinner table against a barrage of disagreement. But the word progress seems to me extremely arbitrary, and our values open to question.

By whose standards – is there an absolute? – do we take it for granted that Cadillacs make a man happier than camels and brick houses bring more harmony to his life than mud huts? Our so called freedom is very precious to us, yet we would chain a nomad to permanent homes, we would bind him to set hours and a regular job (pulling and pushing knobs perhaps), then present him in place of his spear with a neatly furled black umbrella, sombre symbol of respectability, security and convention. We would then feel very pleased with ourselves because we could look at him and say: 'My goodness, how incredibly we have improved his standard of living in the last twenty years!' – taking it completely for granted that that shibboleth of the twentieth century 'high living standard' has, and only can have, one frame of reference.

Meanwhile, though we take his spear away from him we continue to develop the atom bomb. And while we are solemnly teaching him that the killing of twenty or a hundred men in a border clash is uncivilized, we ourselves are busy slaughtering millions in our own wars – and against our very religions and ethics at that! We deplore the cruelty of circumcision, the missionaries especially, yet the Pope himself refused to take a stand against the untold suffering and liquidation of six million Jews! We condemn the African custom of taking several wives simultaneously while for some inconceivable reason we consider it perfectly correct to take (and abandon) several wives in succession ourselves. We teach the African the Christian principle of love and self-denial while we only pay lip-service to it in our own society, partly because such principles are too lofty for us, partly because the goals of our society are completely opposed to it. We give to the African with one hand, and take away and destroy with the other; he has our knowledge, our religion, our comforts, our literature, our music, our art and our medicine; with this we bequeath as well our heritage of lunatic asylums, our broken families, our old-age homes, our prostitutes, our street gangs, our drug addicts, our *sophisticated* cruelty, our obsession with time, our craving for materiality, our corruption, our coronaries, our insomnia – and our wars.

And yet, confusing sophistication with civilization, there are millions of people who would call the two Samburu girls primitives – savages even.

It seems to me that we and they are both equidistant from the golden mean.

I was to be convinced of this yet more strongly when we returned at last to Marsabit. Nine years had passed since that first visit and Monty said I had built up an illusion of 'The Mountain'. I didn't believe this and I was impatient to return.

*

When finally we set off, taking Mandy and Lissa with us this time, I found many significant changes. The macadamized road stretches all the way to the little frontier 'township' of Isiolo now. There is still a barrier across the road, and a sentry on duty, but a pass is no longer required if you are just going as far as Marsabit; nor is it obligatory to go in convoy. A new wide earth road is in the making, and soon the brash new scar across the country will go all the way to Ethiopia. It pushes the scenery back and separates you from it. I felt this especially strongly when we left the burning stones and dry wisps of grass of the Kaisut Desert and began climbing the three thousand feet into the breezy hill tops of the Mountain itself. The wild, tumbling beauty was as I remembered it, but I missed the narrow, winding track that cut deep into the heart of it. And then, as we neared the 'town' itself, we passed a rash of workers' corrugated huts, and yellow bulldozers were scattered across the slopes. The township itself had expanded: a crowd of people, some of them workers from the south, mingled on the dusty earth between the dukas which had now doubled or trebled in number. Some of the new ones were of stone, all of them were ugly. But trade was brisk, so what did any of the rest matter?

CIRCLE VII

I felt heavy hearted, I could hardly believe that already the steel and concrete tentacles of progress were beginning to spread across the remote regions of Kenya's north. But a few moments later I had forgotten the depressing symbols of the twentieth century, for now we had entered a primaeval forest.

The narrow path plunged and dipped between the ancient growth, trees that had been regenerating themselves for a million years. Bark and leaves and lichen glimmered in the shafts of sunlight that sifted through the foliage or hung enmeshed in the leaves like fine golden webs. There were delicate yellow flowers on slender twigs like some Chinese blossom, fine vines were flung like a wild tangle of hair over bushes and liana vines hung down like ropes. Pale green lichen hung from branches like miniature, windblown waterfalls; thick moss blanketed entire branches and barks. Occasionally a bird sang out with a melodic clarity that was almost unearthly. It was as though the forest were enchanted and it held us spellbound.

We drove for an hour along the winding, plunging path. Then, in a clearing, we glimpsed the sort of view that had made of Marsabit an unforgettable place for me: beyond the windblown slopes of the arrogant hills, the burnt plains of the desert three thousand feet below sprawled out towards the horizon, yet we ourselves were lifted way up in the cool green depths of the rain forest. And on the other side, at the foot of the thickly wooded walls of a crater, lay Lake Paradise. Beyond, we could see right across the desert again.

Two elephants were standing at the water's edge, about a thousand feet below us. One was extremely large. A glimpse through the binoculars confirmed that it was indeed Ahmed, the great old tusker. A young male elephant was guarding him. We had picked up a game ranger at Marsabit Game Park headquarters, Guyo by name, a small, thin, quiet man with observant eyes and a sudden, bright smile; it lit his face now as he recognized the elephant. People often spend weeks searching for Ahmed, but there he was awaiting our arrival as it were; we descended into the crater, left the vehicle, and approached closer to him on foot. He stayed by the water for a while, drank his fill, then ambled away from the lakeside and back into the secrecy of the forest.

It was Christmas, and it was white. For in the morning we awoke to a thick mist; it rolled off the water, enmeshing the liana vines and thick foliage of the crater wall that rose sheer behind our tents. Here and there a shadowy pattern of leaves, or the indistinct line of a branch floated in a strange dream world. Figures moving in and out of the mist were dreamlike too – Guyo, Monty, Mandy, Nan, Lissa with her long hair floating in the cloud, enveloped by it, lost to view.... Sometimes the wind lifted the mist momentarily, partially revealing a few grey ripples on the lake, and the black silhouettes of the coots. Or Guyo, silhouetted by the fire, a still, lone form.

We drove down the other side of the Mountain, taking the old route Monty and I had followed to North Horr and Lake Rudolf. The new road had petered out and we jolted along the rough, stoney track once more. Nothing had changed. Here all was sun and sky, hills and stones and space. I felt again the heady feeling of freedom in the restless touch of the breeze, in the surging vastness of the land and the wild strength of the hills.

CIRCLE VII

An old Gabra appeared, spirited out of space. His body was fleshless as a stick, but the skin of his face was drawn smooth across the bones and the full lips curved sweetly, almost like a child; only his eyes were old, old as the earth.

He clambered into the vehicle beside us. I doubt if he had ever ridden in a car before, he covered his old head against the wind, gripping the hand-rail tight in silent protestation against this rattling of his aged bones. When we stopped once more, he shook hands with each of us in turn and in the rolled 'r's and slightly guttural speech of the Gabra, gave us his thanks and his blessings and made his farewells, disappearing into the wilderness whence he came.

We lingered a while, not wanting yet to turn back. Two more Gabra appeared. They asked us for water but they did not take more than two swallows each; water was too precious a commodity to waste – their own or anyone else's. Each of them had that special sort of face that is born out of the timeless distances and the stones: the vision of a prophet and the arrogance of a prince, the stoicism of an ascetic and the watchfulness of a hawk, the face of a man who all his life has possessed only the barest essentials, who has partaken of a minimum of food but drunk his fill of sunlight and space and reaped his share of an African harvest.

In another generation, two at the most, his breed will have died out. Nothing will remain of the tough, independent way of life perfected by these nomads and uncorrupted so far by our own values; little will remain of their land either, for even this, the last bastion of nature, is succumbing to the incursions of the bulldozer and where once there was beauty and silence, there will be flashing steel and towering concrete and screaming supersonic planes. Yet still we continue, still we refuse to draw back, even though we know the inheritance of which we are dispossessing our grandchildren and that it may happen they will one day send up a terrible cry, longing with an unbearable longing to exchange all our mighty progress for one breath of still pure air, for an empty mile and the sound of silence.

Glossary of Swahili Words

Askari	Policeman or Guard
Baharini	By the sea
Baraza	Meeting
Duka(s)*	Small shop
Kanga(s)	African form of women's dress
Kikoi(s)	White loin cloth with coloured border
Manyatta	Masai village
Mganga	Witch-doctor
Moran	Masai word for warrior
Ngalawa(s)	Small dug-out canoe with outriggers
Panga	Matchet, large knife
Pombe	African beer made from grain and bananas
Rungu	Knobkerrie

The 's' is an anglicized form of the plural. In Swahili it is the initial letter that changes, according to the class of noun.